Advanced
Swing
Trading

John Wiley & Sons

Founded in 1807, John Wiley & Sons is the oldest independent publishing company in the United States. With offices in North America, Europe, Australia, and Asia, Wiley is globally committed to developing and marketing print and electronic products and services for our customers' professional and personal knowledge and understanding.

The Wiley Trading Series features books by traders who have survived the market's ever changing temperament and have prospered—some by reinventing systems, others by getting back to basics. Whether a novice trader, professional or somewhere in between, these books will provide the advice and strategies needed to prosper today and well into the future.

For a list of available titles, please visit our Web site at www.Wiley Finance.com.

Advanced Swing Trading

*Strategies to Predict,
Identify, and Trade
Future Market Swings*

JOHN CRANE

WILEY

John Wiley & Sons, Inc.

Published by John Wiley & Sons, Inc., Hoboken, New Jersey.
Published simultaneously in Canada.

All charts used in this manual, unless otherwise identified, are furnished courtesy of FutureSource™.

MetaStock Charts courtesy of Equis International.

For general information on our other products and services, or technical support, please contact our Customer Care Department within the United States at 800-762-2974, outside the United States at 317-572-3993 or fax 317-572-4002.

Wiley also publishes its books in a variety of electronic formats. Some content that appears in print may not be available in electronic books.

For more information about Wiley products, visit our web site at www.wiley.com.

Library of Congress Cataloging-in-Publication Data:

ISBN 0-471-46256-X

Printed in the United States of America.

10 9 8 7 6 5 4 3 2 1

Acknowledgments

This book would never have made it all the way to publication without the helping hands of many individuals. In particular, I am extremely grateful for all the help that I received from Joseph Kellogg, Melissa Hughes, Peggy Anderson, Steve von Furstenrecht, Darren Lalonde, Jaye Abbott, and special thanks to my daughter, Anastasia. All of your contributions to this book are priceless.

I would like to dedicate this book to my wife, Angela, and to my two daughters, Ana and Holli—the three most special people in my world.

J.C.

Contents

Preface

The continual need to expand one's knowledge or to improve an existing idea is an inherent one in all of us. After finishing my earlier book *A Traders Handbook: The Reversal Day Phenomenon* (Traders Library, 1998) I continued to work on my theories of Action/Reaction, with the objective of finding new ways to expand and to improve this unique trading approach. I discovered, or stumbled across (depending on how you look at it), a whole new way of using time, price, and patterns to predict market moves. In this book, I share with you my exciting new discoveries.

This book deals with the Action/Reaction theory by combining price levels, timing methods, and confirmation patterns that strengthen the predictability of future market moves. I take a step-by-step look at the Action/Reaction theory and illustrate how the market goes through a complete and predictable cycle that I call the Reaction cycle. Using this technique, a trader can predict the beginning of a new trend and then project the time and price of the center and end of this new trend.

One of the unique techniques in this book is the method of projecting future prices. I have not seen this technique published before. By using my Action lines and Reaction lines within the Reaction cycle, I illustrate how to project the time and price of major market reversals. This cycle tells the trader if the market is going to make a major turn or if the market is going to make only a small correction against the prevailing trend.

One of the most frequent questions people asked me after reading my earlier book was, "Does this method also work for stocks?" The answer is: Yes, it does! Chapter 15 shows how the Reversal dates work just as well for stocks as they do for futures. Since most of my experience has been in the futures market, the majority of the examples in this book are from futures markets. However, this in no way means that this technique can be used only in the futures markets.

My hope is that the information in this book will increase your awareness of the market's true behavior and serve as a confirmation of your own market analysis.

I offer help throughout every step of your learning process. My specially trained staff is available to answer questions and guide you through the rough spots. You can also follow my daily updates and compare your results with mine. See the end of the book for more information on how to take advantage of this valuable resource.

Introduction

In the latter part of 1999, I was at a small neighborhood gathering. One of the wives at the gathering was giving out stock advice to anyone willing to listen. (I was amazed at how many people were actually listening.) She was telling the group about how well her investment club was doing (the club was a small group of women from her work at a local computer company) and about how she and her husband were moving the majority of their retirement savings into the tech stocks, because the move was just beginning. "This is the new economy," she said. "And if you don't buy now, you will be left behind!"

I remembered thinking about a television program that I had seen just a couple of days before this little gathering. The business channel was profiling a young market analyst and giving him almost celebrity status. For the prior two years, this analyst's stock recommendations had been on target and had registered double-digit returns. He was only 28 and had been in the business for just six years. He was so brash that he predicted the Dow Jones Industrial Average at 15,000 in the next six months.

One of my wife's friends was telling her how her husband would come home during his lunchtime and day trade stocks over the Internet. He was doing so well that he was considering leaving his engineering job.

One of the clients who trades at my firm called me to say that he wanted to put most of his capital into the Nasdaq futures and that he had already moved his retirement account into the tech stocks.

The whole nation was bullish and the stock market was the favorite topic of conversation wherever you went. It seemed everyone had become a stock expert overnight. It was easy money. All you had to do was just buy and hold on for the ride. Whenever the market staged a small correction, the cry was "Buy more," because the market would go back up, as it always had before! This strategy was the only one that most of these new investors knew, and it was the only one they needed. Or so it seemed.

This reminds me of the story told about a time when Joseph Kennedy was having his shoes shined in Grand Central Station. As he was sitting and reading his newspaper, the young man who was shining his shoes told Joe that he had bought some stock for himself, which meant that he now had himself a piece of the American dream. This conversation convinced Joe that the bull market of the 1920s was over. He reasoned, "If the shoe shine boy is in the market, who is left to buy? If everyone is in the market, there is nowhere for it to go but down." The story goes on to tell how Joe Kennedy pulled his money out of the stock market and avoided the disastrous crash of 1929.

Thirteen weeks after the neighborhood gathering, the Nasdaq topped! During the next three weeks, the Nasdaq lost what it had taken more than 20 weeks to gain. It recovered over the following two weeks, but then collapsed again, and traded even lower for the next four weeks. Here we are two years later and the Nasdaq is still down. All the gains made during the runaway bull market have been taken back.

Like many people, the neighbor's wife and husband lost a large percentage of their retirement savings and are no longer speculating in the stock market. I don't hear much about the young market analyst anymore, as the young rising star had never experienced a bear market before. He didn't know how to predict a market that could actually go down. A trader even called me to say that his broker quit out of frustration, because he didn't know how to trade in this type of a market.

Much of this distress and financial loss could have been avoided had investors taken some time and a little effort to educate themselves on market behavior. When all the inexperienced investors were jumping on the bandwagon, the market was actually waving red flags of warning all over the place. Some investors, knowing what to look for, saw these warnings and took action. About the time the market was coming to a climax, I was speaking at a seminar in San Francisco on the Reversal date and Action/Reaction theory (the subject of this book). After the presentation, I was approached by one of the attendees, whom I knew from one of my previous seminars. He pulled out a chart of the Dow Jones index, on which he had applied some of my timing indicators and reversal patterns. Based on this analysis, he said that he had just pulled all his money out of the tech stocks and was going to short the Dow Jones futures. This man is a perfect example for us to emulate. He took the necessary time and effort to educate himself on market behavior and he was rewarded with close to one million dollars in profit. In addition, his education helped him recognize the market top and the need to step out of the market entirely.

In the current "I want everything in a hurry" trading atmosphere, investors and traders have little patience. However, if you study the paths of successful traders from the past and the present, you will find that they have many things in common. The most important of these similarities are patience, discipline, and a willingness to work as hard and as long as it takes to succeed. Successful traders realize that the pathway to continued success comes not from inside information or even from an overabundance of knowledge, but from the understanding of human behavior and how it translates into the market. This formula has not changed since the early 1800s, when U.S. futures trading began on the Midwestern frontier and could probably be traced back as far as 1640, when trading took place in tulip bulb futures.

Jesse Livermore, one of the great traders during the early twentieth century, stated that one of the most important keys to his success as a trader was understanding market behavior and cutting his losses quickly. Jack Schwager, in his book *Market Wizards*, interviewed Paul Tudor Jones, who is possibly one of the most successful traders of our time. Paul Tudor Jones insists that a huge part of his success comes from cutting his losses quickly. If the market is not behaving the way he thinks it should, he gets out.

Of the millions of people involved in speculative markets, only a small percentage spend the time and effort needed to learn how to trade. Although there is no Holy Grail to trading success, there are road maps and warning signs available to guide you toward your desired destination.

I find it interesting to note that new technology (faster computers and more sophisticated software) has not made current traders better or more successful than many of the early traders who used nothing but a pencil and charting paper.

Yes, there are many stories of traders who made a killing off one trade, or maybe even a string of trades. This will always happen, as it is the nature of the markets to offer these types of opportunities. However, you need to be ready to take advantage of these opportunities when they are offered, because the market will take them away quickly. Unfortunately, for every lucky trader there are countless others who are not so lucky. The good news is that long-term success is available to everyone who has desire, dedication, and a strong work ethic.

As I write the introduction to this book, there is a young man from our town getting ready to ski in the Olympics. He and his older brother started to ski when they both were very young. A friend asked the older brother how he felt about his younger brother being an Olympic skier and a top contender for the gold medal. He replied, "I'm a better skier than he is!" When asked why his younger brother made the team and he didn't, he replied, "I quit skiing a long time ago. I got tired of all the work—to me it was not worth all the effort." This statement says volumes about the difference between success and failure. You have to believe the rewards will outweigh the effort.

This book is not meant to be a road-to-riches, no-risk type of book. It is a serious endeavor that will require study and concentration on your part. But as you read through it and study the examples and explanations, you will quickly realize the tremendous value of the information and indicators.

I share with you the indicators used by the gentleman at my San Francisco seminar to determine when it was time for him to exit the market, near the all-time high in the Dow Jones index. In my book, I also introduce you to a trader who achieved the remarkable feat of taking his $100,000 account to over $1,500,000 in six weeks—not just once, but twice in one year. He would wait patiently for the right moment and market setup and then make his move. The one pattern he used so successfully to enter the market is described and illustrated in this book.

This book is about time, price, and patterns, and the overall behavior of the market. It is not meant to be a turnkey system. The methods concentrate on helping you understand market behavior that will enable you to see current market action and know, with a high degree of reliability, what will happen next.

My goal is to provide you with the knowledge and confidence so that you can add what you learn in this book to whatever trading approach you are most comfortable using. Since most of the information in this book is designed to anticipate trend exhaustion or trend reversals, it may appear unconventional to some traders familiar with technical analysis. The Reversal day and Action/Reaction techniques described in this book can be applied to either stocks or commodities. In addition, they work equally well on daily or intraday charts. I will introduce you to the Reaction swing and the concept of the Reaction cycle. I strongly encourage you to apply them both.

In the past few years, many investors have evolved into traders. This is a natural and comparatively easy progression that requires no additional abilities or experience. The current environment of easy access to information and the lure of easy riches has made the growth of trading similar to the Gold Rush in the mid-1800s. This pattern was predictable and glorified by the media. In this book, I present an easy and objective way to determine market direction and identify pending market reversals. Though no person is infallible, I believe learning the methods described in this book will give the trader a tremendous edge, as well as reduce the stress of blindly trading without the knowledge of market behavior. The ability to look at the market and have confidence in your trading decision is worth its weight in gold.

Trading offers one of the last great frontiers of opportunity in today's economy. It is one of the few avenues that offer everyone equal opportunity. There are very few venues where an individual can start with a relatively small bankroll and actually become a millionaire. While I hardly expect all readers of this book to suddenly transform into supertraders, I do believe the information contained in it will open your minds to a new way of looking at the market that will improve your personal trading performance.

CHAPTER 1

Order from Chaos

Have you ever looked at one of those pictures that at first glance seem to be only a hodgepodge of colors, dots, and shapes splashed randomly across the page? Initially, the picture doesn't excite you. However, if you stare at it long and hard enough, it starts to blur and you begin to see an actual picture within the picture. Slowly, a 3-D image begins to take shape and emerge from within the mass of colors and shapes. Once you have seen the image, it is much easier to see each subsequent time you look at the picture. It always seems that there is one person who can see the image immediately. For others, even though it takes more time and effort, the image finally appears. And then there are those people who just can't see it or just don't want to put in the effort.

Initially, a price chart is similar to that hodgepodge picture. It is really nothing but a series of lines and numbers illustrated in a visual form. At first glance, it may not reveal a lot of information. However, with study and experience, a clear picture begins to appear out of this clutter. Price trends start to be seen and chart patterns begin to be identified. With sufficient experience, one can use this information to predict future price movements.

Although the price fluctuations may seem random, they are the result of many forces working together in a very efficient manner. Out of this apparent disorder, one begins to see a market that is moving in a very deliberate pattern, driven by buyers and sellers with different opinions about future prices.

One February afternoon in 1999, I was on a flight traveling from Denver to New York City to attend a meeting with representatives of the New York Mercantile Exchange. I was serving a second term as president of the National Introducing Brokers Association at the time. As I often do during long flights, I pulled out my stack of commodity futures price charts and began to calculate Reversal dates, using a technique that I had developed a few years earlier. Even though the Reversal dates had served me well, I always felt there was more to the picture than I was seeing. I decided to apply a couple of theories that I had been mulling over. After some time, a pattern that I hadn't noticed before began to unfold as clear as day. There on the chart was a distinctive, repetitive pattern. All of a sudden it was very simple.

How many times have you looked at a great idea and been amazed at its simplicity? That is how I felt when I finally noticed what I now call the Reaction cycle. I tried it on numerous other charts and found that it still worked. After testing this new discovery on several commodity charts, I decided to test it on some stock charts. To my amazement and delight, it worked just as well. I became very excited because for the first time I was truly able to understand market behavior.

I now possessed the tool that would allow me to identify the beginning of a major trend, to identify when and where the center of the trend should occur, and to determine the price level and time frame when the trend would be exhausted.

Most of the current technical analysis is just a rehash of discoveries introduced years ago by great trading legends such as W. D. Gann, R. N. Elliott, Allen Andrews, and others. Although their trading approaches were different, the premise of their methodologies was the same. They all believed that there were natural cycles circulating throughout the markets.

Yes, the factors of supply and demand do play a key role in market behavior. However, they do not play the role that most people think. You see, the simplistic law of supply and demand is constantly subjected to a force that is equally powerful, very hard to measure, and infinitely less logical. That force is human emotion. As a result of two emotions that are as old as humanity (greed and fear), most traders have a tendency to overreact to market conditions. When things are going well, traders succumb to greed and overbuy in an effort to maximize profits. When the market is not going their way, fear kicks in, followed by a flurry of selling. These two opposing market forces have been around since the market began and will continue to always be a large factor. Supply and demand may change, but human emotions remain constant.

PRICES LEAD FUNDAMENTALS

The statement that prices lead fundamentals has probably shocked or upset many traders. The fact is that I believe price leads fundamental news in the marketplace. Markets seem to top just when the fundamental news is the most bullish and bottom out when the news or reports are the most bearish. I'm unable to count the number of times traders have asked me, "How can the market be trading higher? We just had a very bearish report." The answer is simple: The price has already discounted the fundamental news. Successful traders are already looking into the future, while novice traders are still trying to trade off past news.

I am not saying that fundamentals do not influence market prices. In fact, they can have a dramatic effect on prices. Market fundamentals of supply and demand are the ultimate decision makers in the marketplace. These forces will move the markets over the long term, while the technical side provides entry and exit signals in the short term.

TECHNICAL ANALYSIS—WHAT IS IT?

Technical analysis is devoted to the internal studies of the markets and not the fundamental (or outside) forces that influence market movement. It looks at the forces that lie within the particular market activity. These forces are generally considered the human qualities and emotions.

It is not important how much a commodity should be worth, but rather how much people are willing to pay for it and the intensity of their belief. In a market based on supply and demand, the intensity of emotion will reveal which one is more powerful—those demanding the commodity or those supplying it.

Each individual has his own reason for buying or selling a commodity. (We do not need to know the reason.) Whatever the reason, it is reflected in the price action with the strongest hand leading the change.

Technical analysis is the study of the actions and net results of all outside influences. The relationship of the two competing forces of supply and demand is reflected in the market by the characteristics of the price action, the nature of the activity, when the action appeared, and how much time it takes to unfold.

The law of supply and demand should and does apply to all free markets. However, sometimes government regulations interfere for short intervals with supply and demand. But, as always, after this interference fails, the markets are given back to the people and the natural laws that govern them.

I find it interesting when a market makes an unexpected large move for no apparent reason, only to be verified by some fundamental news released at a later date.

Jesse Livermore, a famous speculator, once wrote,

Remember there is always a reason for a stock acting the way it does. But also remember the chances are you will not become acquainted with the reason until some time in the future, when it is too late to act on it profitably.

UNIVERSAL LAWS OF PRICE ACTION

It is obvious that universal laws govern all aspects of nature, from the changing seasons to the rise and fall of the tides and right down to the smallest atom of the universe. We accept this to be true. Therefore, can we accept the premise that these laws may affect the actions of man and that under certain conditions he will have similar or repetitive reactions? If this holds true in the markets, then price patterns will repeat themselves as traders react to current patterns in the same way they did to past patterns. Therefore, the past can illuminate the future.

Every trade needs three things in order to successfully identify a correct signal—*time, price, and pattern.* When all three components come together, great things can happen. If you can improve the timing of your entry price, it will enhance *any* trading method. That is what the Reversal date indicator and the Reaction cycle will do for you. *It will tell you the precise day a market will likely react and the level the market needs to be at for it to react. It will even tell you what the market must do to confirm the trade signal.*

This is all based on the market theory that *for every action in the markets there is an equal and opposite reaction.* This means that if you can find the right *action* point in the market, you should be able to predict the *reaction.* Amazingly, you can predict to the exact day when the market will likely reverse. *The key to all of this is the ability to find the end of the initial Action and the beginning of the Reaction.*

This may sound like a complicated and difficult task, especially to those not well versed in technical analysis. However, in reality it is very simple and easy to learn. This methodology is entirely based around one chart pattern that I call the *Reaction swing.* The Reaction swing is the first thing we will learn, as it will lay the groundwork and allow everything else to simply fall into place.

There are many things that help a trader become more successful.

These include commonsense rules and sound techniques. However, I believe that two things are critical and must be possessed before anyone begins to trade in the market. These two things vital to any trader are *knowledge* and *confidence*—knowledge of how the markets work and confidence in the trading approach one has chosen to use. In this book, I give you the knowledge so you know how to identify when a major move in the market is about to begin or end, how to understand what the market is telling you, and how to react to the well-defined patterns. However, you will have to build your own confidence. This is critical because without confidence in your ability to use it, knowledge is useless. Confidence comes from study and practice. The more you see the market react as you anticipate, the more you will believe.

TECHNICAL INDICATORS

There are many technical tools available to traders today—so many, in fact, that it can be confusing for traders as they scamper from one new indicator to the next in an effort to find the one just right for them. New technology has made it easy to develop and test new indicators and has led to a surge of new systems available to the public. It was widely anticipated that new technology would open up the floodgates of prosperity to whoever was willing to pay the price for the system. However, the floodgates did not burst open. The computer made it easier, but not necessarily better.

This overdependence on computer systems is keeping people from learning the basics of trading. To be a successful trader, you need to get back to the basics and learn the characteristics of the market. All markets display certain inherent behavior. Learning to identify and exploit this behavior is essential in becoming a successful trader. It enables you to anticipate the market's movement and react in a purposeful way. Rewards still come to those who are willing to work hard, learn the markets, and anticipate and react to changes quickly. Unfortunately, traders who look for the easy way to riches end up losers. A trader will experience real success only by learning the skills to trade, not by buying the latest system.

LAGGING BEHIND

I started trading in the early 1980s simply by learning to use basic trend line and classic chart patterns, such as head and shoulders, flag and pennant formations, and others. These patterns have been used by traders for years (long before I came along), and still remain very popular today.

Like most traders who initially taste some success, I became thirsty for more knowledge. Therefore, I went in search of more advanced indicators because I was convinced that they would make me more successful. I began to learn more about momentum indicators, such as the Relative Strength Indicator (RSI), stochastics, and moving averages. The purpose of these indicators is to measure the strength of the market and predict when the market is losing or gaining momentum.

Although these indicators have their uses and are very good at supplying valuable information, they should not be used on a stand-alone basis, as their calculations are all based on past information. Consequently, they will often trigger buy or sell signals after the market has already made a substantial move. This causes traders to enter a market when it is overbought or oversold and ready for a correction. The traders then have to decide whether to exit their trades or to sit through what they hope is only a small price correction.

Using these indicators did give me a good idea about the overall trend and strength of a market. This fit well with the teachings found in the majority of the trading books I had read. The so-called trading experts insisted that the only way to be a successful trader was to "take it out of the middle." They described the danger of trying to enter at tops or bottoms, stating that the only safe and sane time to enter a trade is after the trend is established and well on its way. Even though there is a lot of wisdom in this trading philosophy, I always felt like I was starting a 100-yard dash 10 yards behind everyone else.

Using these traditional technical indicators made it easy enough to enter a market in an established trend. However, I had to sit through some large price fluctuations and take on more risk than was necessary. The more I read and the more I traded, the more I knew I wanted to find a different way to analyze the markets. I wanted to find a methodology that would allow me to maximize profits and to reduce risk. This would require a way to enter a trade earlier and exit later or, in other words, catch the turns and improve my timing in the market.

THE SAME, ONLY DIFFERENT

I figured that if I was reading all this information about the right way to trade, then other traders were probably reading and using the same information. We were probably studying the same chart patterns and using the same technical indicators. If the saying was true that "80 percent of traders lose money," I didn't want to look at the market in the same way the 80 percent looked at the market. Therefore, I knew that to truly understand the market, I'd have to start looking at it differently and begin thinking outside the box. I would no longer be able to be content to simply follow the mainstream and trade lagging and late indicators.

This statement reminds me of the picture that was shown to my class when I was in grade school (I'm sure just about everyone has seen this picture). It was a black-and-white drawing of either an old lady in a feathered hat or a young woman with a fancy hairdo (depending how you looked at the picture). When the teacher asked each of us to describe the drawing, some of my classmates said they saw the older lady in the feathered hat while others said it was the young woman. It was only after the teacher pointed out the two different images that we could see both the old lady and the young woman. Naturally, a small percentage of the students could never see either image.

This is a good illustration of how several people can look at the same information and come to many different conclusions. This is actually desirable in the market because it requires different opinions to function. However, I wanted to be able to see the market from a different perspective than the mass majority of traders. Therefore, I had to look outside the box.

In 1989, I had just moved to Eugene, Oregon, from southern California, where I had been working for a large brokerage firm. While in California, I had written some articles on my research about using technical analysis in conjunction with seasonal tendencies in the market. These articles caught the attention of a firm in Chicago. The firm was so impressed with my unique research that they soon asked me to join their research facility in Eugene, Oregon. It was an offer I couldn't refuse.

This firm's research facility was so state-of-the-art for 1989 that it even had its own computer programmer. If I had an idea, Nick, the programmer, would write a program to test the idea.

It was during this time that I stumbled across a significant finding in the markets. I was conducting some extensive research that used cycles to help identify more precise entry and exit points in a seasonal move. While doing this research, I found that one price pattern kept giving me precise turning points in the market. This finding required me to think outside the box because this new way to measure cycles was completely different from the commonly accepted practice in 1989. This recurring price pattern in the market that I uncovered would become the foundation of my Reversal date trading indicator.

From this initial discovery, the Reversal date indicator has evolved into a complete study of the natural movements of the markets. One thing that all the established trading experts had in common was the belief in the concept of time and price working in harmony with the markets. The Reversal date indicator takes this idea one step further as it incorporates price patterns with time and price for an additional confirmation of a trade signal.

This technical approach offers the three key components that I believe are essential for any trade signal—time, price, and pattern. If you can improve the timing of your entry price, you will enhance any trading method (whether it is for stocks or commodities). To be successful in the markets, you don't need extensive knowledge about all the markets you trade or even access to inside information. What you do need and what will go a long way in helping you become a successful trader is to develop a thorough understanding of market behavior.

CHAPTER 2

What Is a Reaction Swing?

Turning a theory into a reality can be a daunting task. When one first reads about the theory of *Action/Reaction*, the first question that probably comes to mind is, "This all sounds great in theory, but can it be applied to real market situations?"

When attempting to solve a problem, the most difficult task is knowing where to start. In this specific case, the problem was how to identify what Action will lead to the *equal and opposite* Reaction.

Markets will always fluctuate and move up and down within a longer-term trend as buying and selling influences price action. It is within this price movement that I found the means to identify where the Action ends and the Reaction begins. Each time the market corrects (trades in the opposite direction of the prevailing trend) and then resumes the current trend, an old cycle ends and a new cycle begins. This pattern occurs over and over in every market, whether one is looking at individual stocks or commodity futures. I call this pattern the *Reaction swing* (see Figure 2.1).

The Reaction swing is a price correction within a trending market, and it can be used as a timing tool for predicting future reversals in a price trend.

The Reaction swing is the key to my methodology. It is where it all begins. If you can find the exact center of a cycle, you can look back at the beginning and then, based on this information, determine where the cycle will go in the future. W. D. Gann once said, "The future is nothing but a reflection of the past."

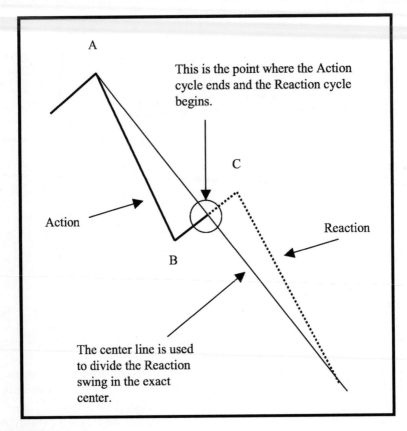

FIGURE 2.1 Action/Reaction

Since the Reaction swing is where the Action ends and the Reaction begins, it marks the center of a repetitive cycle in which the past can project the future. In Figure 2.1, the price movement between B and C is the Reaction swing.

In this chart example, the prevailing trend is down. Midway in the trend, the market trades higher for a few days before turning lower and resuming the downward trend. The price pivot between B and C is a minor price swing against the main trend. Once the market forms a new pivot at C and turns lower, the Reaction swing (B to C) is formed.

Once the Reaction swing is established, you can determine the center of the Reaction swing by drawing a line from the high of the previous Reaction swing, marked as A in this example, through the center of the current Reaction swing. This will divide the Action from the Reaction.

In traditional technical analysis, these chart patterns are called flags or pennants. Usually a trader will look at these patterns as a means to estimate the distance the market should move if and when it breaks out of the pattern. Although this method predicts a good target area, it is limited as it offers only a one-dimensional approach—that of price alone.

A Reaction swing begins and ends with the lowest and highest closing prices—*always use the closing prices.* For example, when a market is trending lower, it will typically make a low closing price before it begins a corrective rally. This is the beginning of a possible Reaction swing. When this corrective rally comes to an end and then resumes the main downward trend, its pivot point is the highest closing price; this is the end of the Reaction swing. The opposite occurs during an upward trending market. Then the Reaction swing starts with the highest closing price and ends up with the lowest closing price before the resumption of the upward trend. Therefore, all you need to know are the dates of the highest closing price and the lowest closing price of the Reaction swing in order to move on to the next step—*projecting future turning points in the market called Reversal dates* (see Figure 2.2).

Reversal dates are future dates where there is a high probability of a Reaction in the market. The majority of the time, this Reaction, on the predicted date, will be a reversal of the market's current trend. The reversal can be at the end of either a long-term price move or a short-term price correction.

However, a small percentage of the time the market will not reverse on the predicted date. Instead, a price pattern will form that I call a continuation pattern. This type of pattern suggests that the market is not ready to reverse, but will continue to trade in the same direction as the current trend. This usually occurs when the market has been in a consolidation pattern (trading sideways). On the predicted date, the market will generally break out of the consolidation pattern and continue the trend. Both the reversal and continuation patterns offer extremely important information to a trader.

REVERSE COUNT

The key to predicting a trend reversal is the reverse count. The reverse count is a count of price periods backward in time. The reverse count counts backward in time from the beginning of the current Reaction swing to the beginning of the previous Reaction swing. (This is the same whether in an advancing or a declining market.)

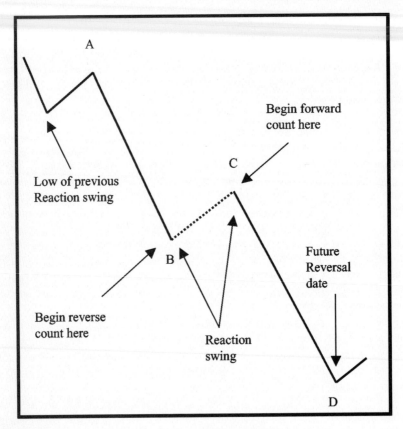

FIGURE 2.2 Reaction Swing—Reverse and Forward Count

Reverse counts go back successively to the beginning of the prior Reaction swing, and can continue back to the respective high or low of the entire new trend. Please note that when a holiday falls on a trading day, it is counted as a regular trading day even though there is no bar for that day on the price chart.

FORWARD COUNT

The forward count is simply the Reaction swing's reverse count applied forward in time. The forward count begins with the first period after the end of the Reaction swing and goes forward in time the same number of periods that the reverse count went backward. Remember, the end of the

Reaction swing in an uptrend is the lowest period close of the downward price correction, and in a downtrend it is the highest period close of an upward price correction.

END OF A REACTION SWING

One can first suspect the end of a Reaction swing when the closes of two consecutive periods move away from the high pivot point (in a downward trend) or low pivot point (in an upward trend) of the Reaction swing and continue in the direction of the main trend. Another way to determine the end of a Reaction swing occurs when the support or resistance line that connects the highs or lows of the Reaction swing is broken by a price move back in the direction of the main trend. Finally, one knows for certain that the Reaction swing is over when the respective high or low close at the beginning of the Reaction swing is exceeded by the price movement in the direction of the main trend.

It is not necessary to draw a line through the center of the Reaction swing when using it to project future Reversal dates. In order to project future Reversal dates, you only need to know the date of the highest closing price and the date of the lowest closing price. Seven rules for this process *in a downward trending market* are:

1. Identify a Reaction swing. The beginning of a Reaction swing will be the period with the lowest closing price prior to a corrective rally.

2. Start on the first day before this lowest close; consider it as day one and count each day going backward.

3. Continue to count each day all the way back to the low at the beginning of the previous Reaction swing. (It is important to remember to count back to the lows in downward trending markets.) This is called the reverse count.

4. If a holiday falls on a trading day, it must be counted even if the market was closed.

5. Now, go to the end of the Reaction swing (in a downward trending market it is the day with the highest closing price) to complete the forward count.

6. Begin with the first day after this highest close and count forward the same number of days equal to the reverse count. For example, if the reverse count to the previous low was 15 days, count forward 15 days.

7. Mark this date as the next potential Reversal date.

Note: Reverse the rules in an advancing market.

COMMON MISTAKES

The most common mistakes that occur while using this trend reversal tool are usually the result of human errors—miscounting periods, misidentifying starting or ending periods of Reaction swings, misinterpreting a series of price bars as a Reaction swing, or trying to identify Reaction swings within trading ranges.

Misinterpreting a series of price bars as a Reaction swing may happen when you forget, for example, that the Reaction swings in a declining market are supposed to slant up, or that the Reaction swings in an advancing market are supposed to slant down. In other words, the group of price periods you identify as a Reaction swing are slanting the wrong way. Remember that a Reaction swing is a price correction within a trending market.

Learning to correctly identify Reaction swings is vital when projecting future Reversal dates in the market. The next few examples will better demonstrate the identification process as it is applied in real market conditions. If you do not completely understand this process, go back and review this chapter and work through the examples before moving on to the next step. Without a complete understanding of the Reaction swing, the following chapter will not make sense.

Take a look at the April Live Cattle example shown in Figure 2.3. The market makes a top at A and then trades lower for several days before it stops trading lower at point B. The market makes a short-term low at B before trading higher. This short-term rally will last for three days and is against the stronger downward trend. After topping out at C, the market continues the downward trend. Once it is evident that the market has turned lower and will continue the current downward trend, the Reaction swing has been formed. Let's review the Reaction swing in Figure 2.3.

Point B is the beginning of the Reaction swing. Notice the closing price? It is the lowest closing price before the market begins the upward corrective swing. The end of the Reaction swing is marked C. Notice the closing price? It is the highest closing price before the market turns lower and continues the current downward trend. The closing prices are very important because they determine the beginning and the end of the Reaction swing. Remember, *always use the highest closing price and the lowest closing price.*

Figure 2.4 shows another example of a Reaction swing in a downward trend, this time in Corn futures with reverse count and forward count.

Note: In a downward trending market, the Reaction swing begins at the lowest closing price and ends at the highest closing price (in these two examples, the Reaction swings are identified by points B and C. The reverse is true in an upward trending market.

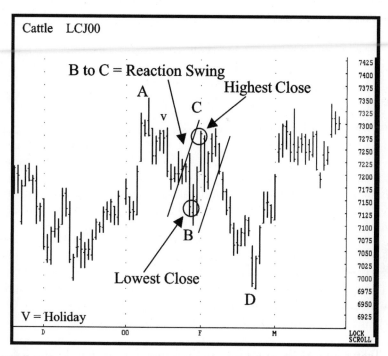

FIGURE 2.3 Reaction Swing in Downward Trend (Live Cattle)

1. From the highest close at A the Live Cattle trade lower and post a low close at B. Point B is the beginning of the Reaction swing.

2. On February 1, 2000, three days after the low close at B, the Live Cattle post a high close at C that completes the Reaction swing.

HOW TO CONFIRM THE REACTION SWING

Again we will answer the question, "How do I know when the Reaction swing is confirmed?" We do this because the Reaction swing is central to this method. There are a couple of ways to confirm a Reaction swing. If the end of the Reaction swing is a high close (this would happen when the overall trend of the market is down), wait until the market closes lower for two days following the high close. The opposite is true in an uptrend, when the end of the Reaction swing would be a low. Another way to confirm the Reaction swing is to wait for the market to trade below the beginning low of the Reaction swing in a downward trending market. The opposite is true for an upward trending market.

Now that the Reaction swing from B to C has been identified as seen in the previous examples, what does it mean, and how can it be used? The Reaction swing will be used to project forward into the future to determine

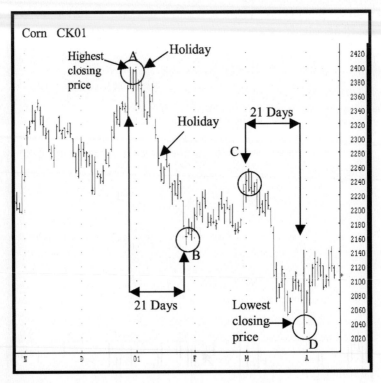

FIGURE 2.4   Reaction Swing in Downward Trend (Corn)—Reverse and Foreseen Count

1. The Corn hits a major high at A that leads to a new downward trend.

2. After a low is established at B, Corn trades higher against the current trend. This market retracement ends at C, which completes the Reaction swing (B to C).

3. The reverse count from B to A equals 21 days. (Remember to count the two holidays.) The forward count of 21 days to D pinpoints the lowest closing price of the entire downward price move.

where *price* and *time* will converge. This is a natural cycle that many traders claim exists, while others say it does not. I will let you make up your own mind. In the meantime, let's take a closer look at some examples to see how the Reaction swing is used.

The main use of the Reaction swing is to identify the center of a price movement in the market. By locating the center, I can look back in time and price and use that information to project forward in time and price. It seems so simple, yet it is a powerful and effective tool. Once I have identified the Reaction swing I do what I call a reverse count.

Reverse Count

In Figure 2.5, the beginning of the Reaction swing is the lowest close, marked B; you simply count backward toward the high at A. To do this,

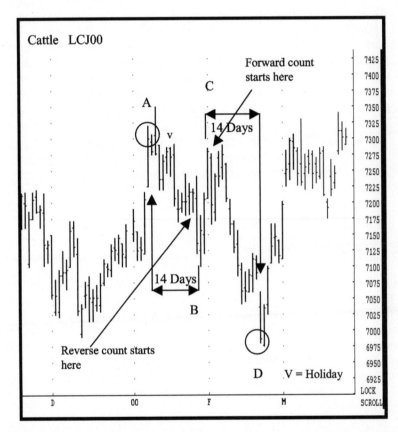

FIGURE 2.5 Reaction Swing in Downtrend (Cattle)—Reverse and Forward Count

1. Begin the reverse count at the first price bar to the left of the lowest closing price, marked B.

2. Count the days from B back to and including the highest closing price at A. Remember to count one day for the holiday, marked V. The reverse count equals 14 days. (Note: You count to A because it is the last high in the upward trend.) Begin the forward count on the first price bar to the right of the highest closing price, marked C. Counting forward 14 days projects a Reversal date on February 22, marked D.

start at the first bar to the left of B and count each bar back to and includ-ing A. (The V on the chart represents a holiday that occurred during the trading week. Holidays are counted just like trading days and therefore are included in the reverse count. Weekends, though, are not counted in the reverse count.) This reverse count should equal 14 bars.

Forward Count

On the same chart, the end of the Reaction swing is marked C. Point C is the highest closing price before the market starts trending lower. Begin-ning at the first bar to the right of C, count forward 14 bars. Remember this number. (This is the same as the reverse count.) You will notice that the 14th bar is the exact lowest close of the move.

This example demonstrates a market that is in perfect balance. It also shows how the Reaction swing helps to find the exact center of the market move. By having this information in advance, you would have known that the market had 14 more days of downward movement from point C before a Reversal date was due. This is crucial because it would have allowed you to know when to look for the end of the current downtrend and the begin-ning of a new market trend.

UPTRENDING MARKET

It is time to apply what we've learned to an uptrending market. We'll use the chart of April Live Cattle shown in Figure 2.6 to find the Reaction swing in a market that is trending higher. In this example, the market makes a series of higher highs and higher lows. Thus it is an upward trending market. The highest close at B is the beginning of the Reaction swing. Notice that B is the highest closing price before the market turns lower and trades against the current trend. The lowest closing price, C, is the end of the Reaction swing. Therefore, the price swing of B to C is the Reaction swing.

Starting with the first bar to the left of B, you begin the reverse count. In this case the reverse count will stop at the highest close marked A. Why, you ask? When the market is trending upward, as in this example, you al-ways count back to the highest closing price of the previous Reaction swing. (In a downward trending market, you always count back to the low-est closing price of the previous Reaction swing.)

The reverse count from B to A equals 19. Now for the forward count. Count forward 19 bars, starting with the first day to the right of the lowest

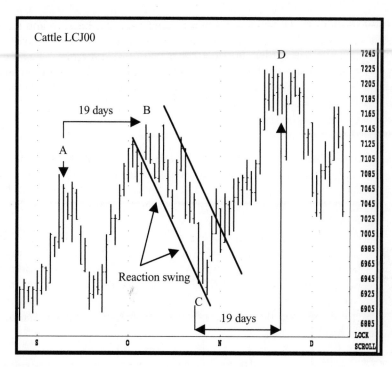

FIGURE 2.6 Reaction Swing—Uptrending Market

1. The Live Cattle market makes a high close at 71.35 (B) before trading lower. After making a low close at 69.30 (C) Live Cattle completes the Reaction swing and resumes the upward trend.

2. The reverse count from B back to the highest close at A equals 19 days. (Remember, in an upward trending market the reverse count begins with the day to the left of the highest close of the Reaction swing and counts back to the high close of the previous Reaction swing. The opposite is true in a downward trending market.)

3. The forward count of 19 days from C projects a Reversal day of November 19, point D.

close marked C. This takes you to D. As you see on this chart, the upward trend ends 19 days after the low close at C.

TIME OR PRICE

This brings me back to a subject that I mentioned earlier—*time, price, and pattern*. I will deal with pattern later. For now, I want to talk about only time and price. The question most asked of me is, "Which one has the most influence on the market? Which one is the leader?" Many would argue that price is the leader; however, this example is a good illustration that shows time as the leader. The price movement from C to D ends when the time is up, *not when a price target is met.* Even though the reverse count of 19 days is not in a straight line, it still projects that 19 days in the future is the end of the time cycle.

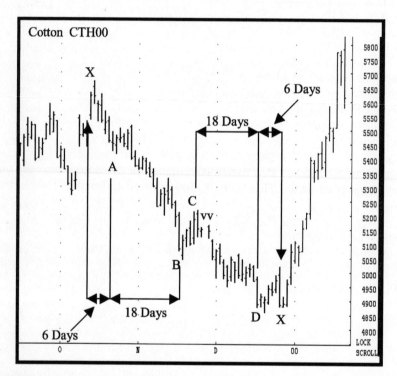

FIGURE 2.7 Extending the Count

1. The Reaction swing is marked as B to C.

2. The reverse count from B to A equals 18 days. Continue the count back to X, the last high in the upward trend, to add six more days.

3. Counting forward 18 days projects a Reversal date of December 16, marked D. Six trading days later, another low occurs on the projected Reversal date of December 27, marked X. See how the Reaction swing (B to C) was the exact center of the move from the high X to the low X.

EXTENDING THE COUNT

The previous examples took the reverse count back to the previous Reaction swing and then used that same number to count forward. Now you may be asking, "Can you go back any further than one Reaction swing using the reverse count?" Yes, you can! You can continue the count back further than one Reaction swing and use these calculations to project future Reversal dates. Let's look at an example.

In Figure 2.7, the Reaction swing is marked B to C. The lowest closing price at B is the beginning of the Reaction swing, and the highest closing price at C is the end of the Reaction swing. The reverse count back to the beginning (or the lowest closing price) of the previous Reaction swing is marked A.

Counting the bars from B to A equals 18 bars. Now, just for fun, continue the reverse count six more trading days, back to the highest closing price, marked X on the chart. This comes to 24 bars. (You count to X because it is the last high in the upward trend.)

Now, complete the forward count starting at the end of the Reaction swing, marked C. Remember to add two bars for the holidays, marked VV. Eighteen bars later, the March Cotton makes a new low and closes at the projected low, marked D. It then trades higher for five days before the market drops once again. This time, it closes lower and makes the contract low on the 24th bar—right on schedule as the Reversal date predicted.

It is very important that you understand how to identify a Reaction swing and how to apply the concept of the reverse/forward count before moving on. Everything is based on this foundation. If you have questions you can call my office at 1-800-831-7654. Specially trained representatives are ready and willing to help.

CHAPTER 3

"Swing Trading" the Reaction Swing

In the late 1990s, stock traders discovered something that commodity futures traders had known for years—volatility offers opportunity. While commodity traders were trading market swings on a short-term basis, stock investors looked only for the long-term investments. The idea was to make money by holding onto a stock for several months or years. To a commodity trader, a long-term trade was two to three weeks and sometimes less. Stocks were considered only for the sophisticated investors, while commodity futures were for the gamblers. Times have changed.

When I first started trading in the late 1970s, investors got excited if the Dow Jones Industrial Average had a 30-point daily range. Currently, a 100-point daily trading range is more the norm. Suddenly, individual stocks are experiencing wide trading swings never seen before. The lure of fast money has brought a new breed of trader into the stock-trading arena. Instead of the traditional investment philosophy of buy and hold for the long term, short-term trading has turned investors into traders. They have brought with them a whole new short-term trading style called swing trading.

New technology and the easy access to a vast amount of information have captivated the imaginations of many novice traders who have fallen into the easy money trap. Unaware of the risks associated with this type of trading, many of the new wave of traders have ended up as trading casualties.

For years, futures traders referred to "swing trading" as a trading strategy that held positions for one to five days. The idea was to capitalize on the short-term cyclical swings occurring within an existing trend. Traders would isolate recurring patterns to trigger buy and sell signals.

New traders would go in search of information that would give them the edge over the rest of the trading world. They would usually begin by memorizing traditional chart patterns such as flags, pennants, and wedges. Naturally, every other trader used these same patterns as well. Most traders did not take the time to study the underlying mechanics of the market in order to understand what created the trading opportunities in the first place.

Complete books have been written that are dedicated to the swing-trading concept. These books describe complicated technical strategies and techniques for short-term traders. Often these techniques require the trader to be glued to a quote machine for the entire trading day. This is okay for some people, but others have to work for a living and cannot be in front of a quote screen all day.

There were and still are many successful traders using this trading approach. Some have claimed ownership of chart patterns and entry and exit strategies. Their success is usually the result of hard work, experience, and their ability to recognize changing market conditions so that they can stay ahead of the crowd.

Many of the chart patterns used by swing traders are masked within the commonly used chart patterns. Unfortunately, as many of these patterns are hard to find and identify, only the most seasoned traders can easily use them. In addition, most swing traders concentrate on and use several patterns. The end result is that the novice trader becomes overwhelmed and frustrated.

The essential ingredients required for swing trading have been around for decades. Today's traders experience the same emotions that traders experienced 50 years ago. As long as human behavior remains the same, market behavior will be the same. As a result of this natural phenomenon, every market (whether in stocks or commodities) offers swing-trading opportunities.

Every trader dreams of having a reliable pattern that can condense the vast amount of market information into a simple, easy-to-use trading strategy. The *Reaction swing* offers just that—a reliable, simple trading strategy that is easy to recognize and implement. Its entry and exit rules are well defined; therefore, the trader knows precisely when and where to enter and exit the market.

As the Reaction swing is easy to recognize, you can quickly scan several markets, place entry orders and protective stops, and then go about your day while your trading plan is in place. Although you can choose to spend the day monitoring each and every move in the market, the best news is that you don't have to!

TIME AND PRICE

My grandfather was the justice of peace of a small town in Idaho. As a small boy, I can remember sitting on the front porch when people would come to pay their traffic fines and conduct other legal business. They would come at all hours of the day and on any day of the week. It seemed like everyone knew him and liked him. I once asked, "Grandpa, how come these people don't get mad at you for making them pay fines?" Grandpa looked at me with his knowing eyes and answered, "Because I keep it simple; that way it makes it easy for everyone to understand. It just works better that way." My grandfather was a very smart man. I believed him then, and I still believe him today. Simple really is better.

The previous chapter described the Reaction swing. This pattern is easily identified on any chart of any market, whether it is in stocks or commodities. It works just as well on intraday charts as it does on daily charts. Now I'm going to share with you another application for the Reaction swing.

The rules for swing trading with the Reaction swing are simple. These easy-to-follow rules are outlined in the following steps:

First, as you need to verify when and where to enter a market, wait for a Reaction swing to form. A Reaction swing must contain three days (this includes the high close and low close).

Second, after a market has completed a Reaction swing, you can determine the pivotal price that confirms a possible swing trade. This key price will be the center of the Reaction swing.

To do this, subtract the low price of the Reaction swing from the high price of the Reaction swing (this can only be done once the market correction has ended) and then divide this number by 2. Now you have a number that is 50 percent of the Reaction swing. Either adding this divided number to the low price of the Reaction swing or subtracting it from the high price of the Reaction swing gives you the price at the center of the Reaction swing. I call this the *trigger price*. When the market reaches this price after the market correction has ended, it triggers the buy or sell stop and the trade is entered.

Third, using the trigger price, trades are made as follows:

For a sell signal in a declining market, place a sell stop at the trigger price (again, this is the 50 percent number as calculated in the preceding step). When the Reaction swing is complete and the market turns lower to resume the downward trend, the sell stop will be triggered as it passes through the trigger price. Once the position has been entered, place a protective stop above the resistance level or high of the Reaction swing.

For a buy signal in an advancing market, place a buy stop at the trigger price (again, this is the 50 percent number as calculated earlier). When the

Reaction swing is complete and the market turns higher to resume the upward trend, the buy stop will be triggered as the market passes through the
trigger price. Once the position has been entered, place a protective stop
below the support level or low of the Reaction swing.

Now that you have determined the entry point, you can predict a target price. To project the price target in a downward trending market as
shown in Figure 3.1, subtract the low price at B from the high price at A.

Next subtract the difference between A and B from the high at C. This
gives you a potential target price at D.

To determine the time duration of the swing trade, you will do a reverse count. Count backward from the low at B back to the high at A.
Next, count forward the same number of days from the high at C. This
identifies the maximum amount of time you should be in this position. You

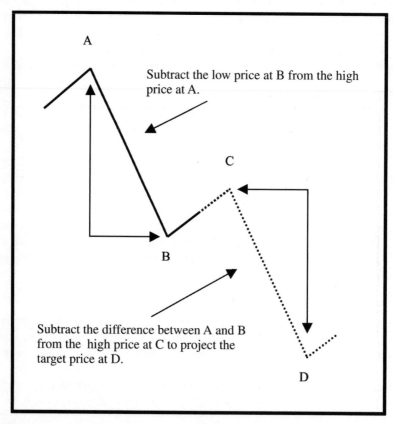

FIGURE 3.1   Action/Reaction—Target Price

should offset or exit the trade at the target price or on the date projected by the forward count—whichever occurs first.

To protect against any surprise or adverse market swings, follow the market down or up with your protective stops. The levels to which one moves the protective stops are up to the individual trader's own discretion. Every trader has a different risk tolerance. Initially, I'd recommend moving the protective stop price to your entry level when the market trades past the beginning of the Reaction swing. In addition, the closer the market gets to the target date or to the price target, the closer I move the protective stops. *Money management is and always will be the most important aspect of successful trading.*

You will see in the following examples that the old rule of thumb for swing trading no longer applies: You can hold a position for longer than one to five days and still take advantage of the short-term market swings. This strategy can be applied to any time frame—from daily charts all the way down to five-minute charts. Let's look at the April Live Cattle chart (Figure 3.2) as a candidate for a swing trade (we used this chart in the previous chapter).

In Chapter 2, you identified the Reaction swing as B to C. As soon as you have determined that this is the Reaction swing, you want to find the

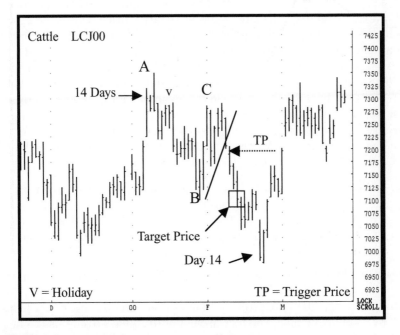

FIGURE 3.2 Swing Trade—Target Price and Time

trigger price of this Reaction swing. The trigger price is the price where I feel that the odds of confirming the Reaction swing and the continuation of the major trend are the strongest. If the correction is indeed over and the Reaction swing is confirmed, the momentum of the market will return to the major trend. This is the ideal situation for a swing trader.

In the April Live Cattle chart, you calculate the center of the Reaction swing in four steps:

1. Subtract the low of 71.20 (B) from the high of 72.85 (C) to get a difference of 1.65 points.

2. Divide 1.65 by 2 to get a total of .825.

3. Subtract .83 (I round up) from the high of 72.85 and you get a price of 72.02 as the center of the Reaction swing.

4. Place a sell stop at 72.02. When the market passes through this price the sell stop is triggered and you are short the Cattle at 72.02.

The next step is to determine the maximum possible time span of the trade. First, complete the reverse count from B to A—this equals 14 days. Next, do the forward count of 14 days from C. (Remember, the reverse count begins on the day to the left of B and the forward count begins on the day to the right of C.) You now know that the maximum possible time to remain in the trade is 14 days following the high of the Reaction swing.

Next, it's time to calculate the possible target price. This is the process used to calculate Reversal dates. The process involves the theory of Action/Reaction—for every action in the markets there is an equal and opposite reaction. This means that the price action leading into the Reaction swing should equal the price action following the Reaction swing. Therefore, let's see how the theory fits in this example. First, subtract B from A. The high at A is 73.20 and the low at B is 71.20. When subtracted, the difference equals 2.00 points. Next, subtract this difference from the end of the Reaction swing (C). When you subtract 2.00 points from the high price at C, you get a target price of 70.85.

1. In Figure 3.2, as soon as B to C is confirmed as a Reaction swing, calculate the center of the Reaction swing: C (72.85) − B (71.20) = 1.65; 1.65 divided by 2 = .825; C (72.85) − .83 = 72.02. The center works out to be 72.02—place a sell stop at this price. The sell stop is filled on the first down day.

2. Now, calculate the projected target price (A − B = 2.00 points; C − 2.00 points is the target price).

3. Finally, calculate the projected target time. The reverse count from B to A equals 14 days. The forward count of 14 days from C is the target time or the projected Reversal date.

This information provides both time and price for the swing trade. The April Live Cattle reaches the target price on the ninth day to close the short position. If the price had not reached the target price by the 14th day, you would exit the trade.

After completing these simple steps, you have all the necessary information to complete your swing-trading plan of action.

As soon as the short position has been entered at 72.02, place the protective stop just above the high of the Reaction swing (C). This should provide good resistance. If this is a true Reaction swing, the high should not be tested again.

You have just calculated the time and price for the swing trade in Live Cattle. The sell stop of 72.02 is hit on the first day following the pivot at C. Based on the reverse count and forward count, you can expect the Cattle to trade sideways or lower for the next 14 days. The plan is to exit the position at the target price of 70.85 or on the 14th day, whichever one comes first.

The next step in your swing-trading plan is extremely important. It provides you with protection in the case of an adverse price move against your position. Once the Cattle have traded below the previous low or the beginning of the Reaction swing (B), move the protective stop down to the entry price. From this point on, move the protective stop down as the price drops.

Since every trader has a different risk tolerance, this is done at the discretion of the trader.

On the ninth day of the trade, the April Cattle reach the target price of 70.85 to close out the short position. The Cattle hit the price level before the time runs out. This is illustrated in Figure 3.2.

As I have gone into great detail explaining the swing-trading process in this example, I will keep my explanations brief for the remaining examples.

GO WITH THE FLOW

Successful swing trading depends on entering with the direction of market momentum. The market spends the majority of its time trading sideways in congestion patterns. Real profits are made when the market breaks out of these congestion areas and moves quickly to the next level of congestion. Therefore, any strategy used to enter the market should be designed to go with the momentum flow. In other words, trade with the trend.

There are many ways to identify a trend—they are too numerous to mention here. This book uses the Reaction swing to determine the current

trend direction. Simply put, a bullish trend is defined as price movement
with higher highs and higher lows. When the market fails to make a higher
high, it foreshadows weakness and signals a possible trend change. The
opposite is true for a bearish trend. The market is in a downward trend as
long as the market continues to make lower lows and lower highs. The
chart example using the September T-Bonds (Figure 3.3) illustrates swing
trading in a bullish trend.

September T-Bonds

In mid-May, the T-Bonds post a low at 98-11 before rebounding over the
next four days. In late May, the T-Bonds trade to another low at 98-13 (A);

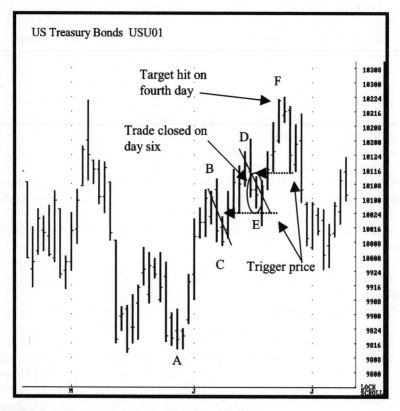

FIGURE 3.3 Swing Trade—U.S. T-Bonds in Uptrend
1. B to C is the first Reaction swing—the trigger price is 100-21.
2. The first swing trade is closed at 101-21 on day 6 of the trade.
3. D to E form the second Reaction swing. The trade is entered at the trigger
price of 101-11. The T-Bonds reach the target price of 102-15 before the time expires.

thus, they test the previous low of 98-11 but do not trade below it. T-Bonds then stage a quick rally off the secondary low (A) and trade above the previous high. This signals a trend change in the T-Bonds. (The market makes a higher low and a higher high that reverses the trend and the market momentum to bullish).

The first Reaction swing forms when the T-Bonds hit a high pivot point at 101-04 (B) and then turn lower. Three days later, the T-Bonds post a low pivot at 100-06 (C) and then turn higher. This confirms the end of the Reaction swing. The center of the Reaction swing is 100-21. This price is used as a buy stop trigger price to enter the bullish swing trade.

You can quickly determine the target price by subtracting the low of 98-13 (A) from the high of 101-04 (B). The difference is 2-23. This difference is used to project the target price by adding it to the low of 100-06 (C). The price target is 102-29.

Now, perform the reverse count from B to A. The count is six days. Project the count forward six days to point D. You hold the long position until it reaches the target price of 102-29 or exit on the sixth day, whichever comes first.

Finally, implement the most important part of the trading plan—the protective stop. When the trade is filled, place the protective stop under the low of the Reaction swing (C). As soon as the market trades above the high of the Reaction swing, move the protective stop to the entry price. This is very important and should not be ignored. *Remember, good discipline and money management separates the winners from the losers.* Now that the trading plan is in place, you can sit back and wait for the trade to unfold.

The T-Bonds trade higher over the next four days, but on the fifth day they reverse and drop though the protective stop to close the trade at the entry price of 100-21.

However, this price action forms a new Reaction swing marked D and E. Since the trend is still bullish, it is time to plan the next potential swing trade.

The center of the Reaction swing is 101-11, the target price is 102-15, and the time duration is four days. The T-Bonds complete the Reaction swing and hit the trigger price to enter a long position at 101-11. On the fourth day of the trade, the T-Bonds hit the target price of 102-15 (F).

September S&P 500

In late May, as shown in Figure 3.4, the September S&P 500 peaks at 1326. For the next three months, the market drifts lower. Although there is not a significant trend, there are seven ideal swing-trading opportunities.

On May 30, the September S&P 500 trades to a low of 1258. That is just below the previous low made two weeks earlier. The S&P rebounds from this low to rally over the next four days before finally topping out at 1297.50 on June 5. This new lower low followed by a lower high has signaled a change of trend in the S&P, from bullish to bearish. In addition, the newly formed Reaction swing alerts you to a possible swing trade.

The first in this series of swing trades unfolds on the S&P in Figure 3.4.

The first sell signal occurs at the trigger price of 1277.75. Once filled, the market momentum carries the S&P lower into the scheduled target day. The trade is closed at 1252.80 on the sixth day from the end of the Reaction swing (C). The result is a gain of 24.95 points. (One point in the S&P is worth $2.50.) The S&P trades lower on the following day. It drops into a low pivot (D) that begins another market correction or Reaction swing.

In Figure 3.5 a Reaction swing is formed at D to E. The trigger price is

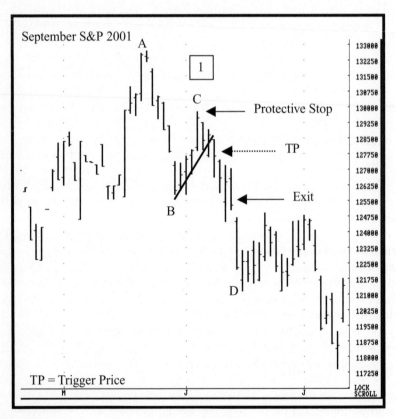

FIGURE 3.4   First Swing Trade in September S&P

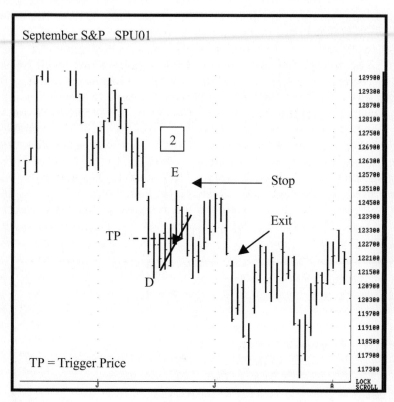

FIGURE 3.5 Second Swing Trade in September S&P

calculated and placed in the market. Once filled, the protective stop is placed above the high (E). When the price moves below the low of the Reaction swing (D), the protective stop is moved to the entry price (the trigger price). Unfortunately, the price turns on the third down day and trades higher into the protective stop. The protective stop is hit, resulting in a break-even trade. Fortunately, this price action forms a third Reaction swing that provides another swing-trading opportunity on July 2.

As shown in Figure 3.6, the trigger price for the third swing trade is filled at 1229.75. The target price is 1209.25 and the time duration is four days from the high close of the Reaction swing. The short sell is triggered on the second down day. On the third day, the S&P opens lower and continues lower for the remainder of the day. The market drops enough to hit the target price and close the short position at 1209.25. This trade has lasted for three days and was closed for a potential gain of 20.50 points.

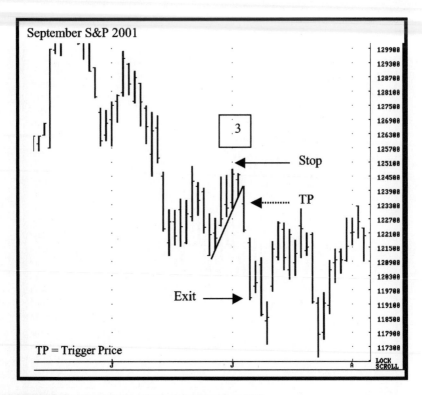

FIGURE 3.6   Third Swing Trade in September S&P

This is the type of swing trade we like, as the market drops quickly and never has an open trade loss.

The fourth trade, shown in Figure 3.7, is set up following a high pivot on July 13. The trigger price is 1199.95. The target price is 1151.90, and the time span is six days. Whether this trade would have been entered is up to the individual trader, as the trigger price is not hit until the sixth day. If taken, this trade offers the potential for a nice gain. The short trade would have been entered at the trigger price of 1199.95 and closed at the end of the sixth day at 1192. The potential gain is 7.95 points.

As shown in Figure 3.8, the fifth swing trade begins at the high pivot point on August 2 as the market reverses after marking a high of 1232.50. The trigger price is 1200.60 with a target price of 1169.80 and a duration of seven days. The short position is entered on the third down day and exited

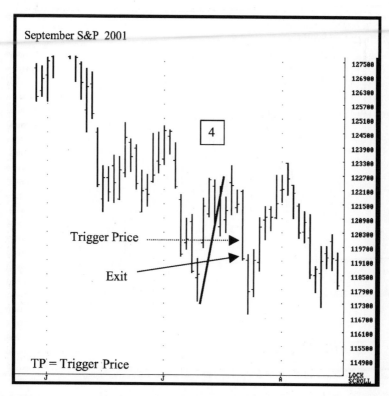

FIGURE 3.7 Fourth Swing Trade in September S&P

at 1192.50, at the close of the seventh day. This is another successful swing trade that offers a potential gain of just over 8 points.

A sixth Reaction swing then forms that provides a sixth swing trade. The trigger price for the sixth trade is at 1184.40, with a target price of 1136.50 and a duration of four days. The trade is offset at the close of the fourth day at 1165.50—a potential gain of 18.90 points.

Two days later, the S&P posts a low close followed by a three-day rally to form a new Reaction swing. This setup creates another potential swing trade—number seven in this trend shown in Figure 3.9. The trigger price to activate the short swing trade is at 1172.50. The target price is 1142.50, and the duration is five days. After the trigger price is filled, the target price is hit on the third day following trade entry. This closes the trade for a potential gain of 30.00 points—another tremendous swing trade!

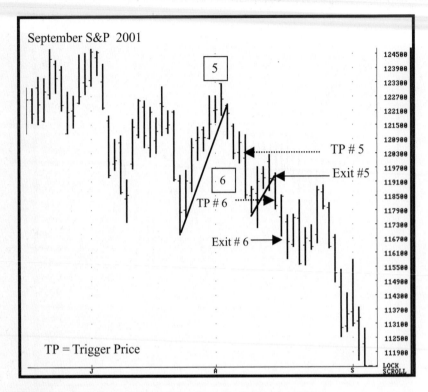

FIGURE 3.8   Fifth and Sixth Swing Trade in September S&P

THE TWO-DAY RULE

My father once said to me, "More is not always better. To get the best from life, you should look for quality, not quantity." He was trying to give me a life lesson, one that I could grab onto to help guide me through the hard times. However, being young, I had no idea what he was talking about at that time.

You've just been shown several examples of swing trades in the S&P 500 and T-Bonds. I showed you all of those examples to demonstrate the versatility of the Reaction swing. These swing-trade patterns occur every day and in all markets. Therefore, if it is trading action you're after, the Reaction swing will provide it. Apply the rules as defined, being sure to practice proper risk management, and you will always be involved in trading action.

I know now what my father was trying to teach me: It is not the quantity of trades that will make you a successful trader, but the quality of

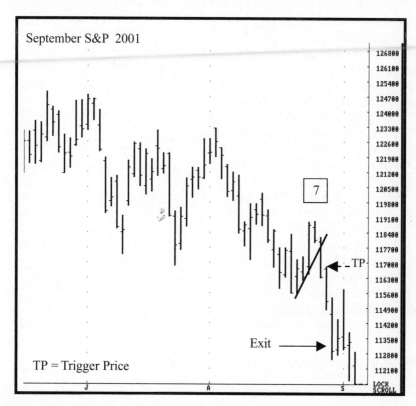

FIGURE 3.9   Seventh Swing Trade in September S&P

trades. It is the ability to find the cream-of-the-crop trades that separates the best from the rest. Why trade a large number of questionable patterns when you can trade less and with a higher degree of success probability? By following the Two-Day Rule, you can trade less and better.

Identifying a Reaction swing can be easy; they are found in virtually every market. However, not all Reaction swings are created equal. When it comes to swing trading, some are better than others.

Utilizing the Two-Day Rule is very simple (this is in harmony with the theme of this chapter). This rule helps with the early identification of a possible Reaction swing before it is confirmed.

The criteria for the Two-Day Rule are simple. If a market is trending higher, you look for a pivot high that is followed by two trading days closing lower than the opening price. (If the market is trending lower, you would look for a pivot low that is followed by two trading days closing higher than the opening price.) When you see this pattern, regard it as a possible swing trade for the next trading session. As I have previously outlined, for a market correction in an uptrend, take the high pivot price and subtract from it the low of the second low-close day; then divide the difference by two. This will determine the center of the price swing—your trigger price. Now that you have the trigger price, place a buy stop (as the trend is up) at the trigger price for the next trading session.

Unfortunately, the Two-Day Rule will keep you out of some profitable swing trades. For example, of our previous seven swing trades in the S&P 500, six were profitable and one just broke even. However, only four of these swing trades met the criteria of the Two-Day Rule. (Note: The unprofitable trade did not.) Therefore, by trading only the swing trades that fit the Two-Day Rule, one would have missed some potential profit.

This is where individual traders will have to decide for themselves whether they want quality or quantity. Although there is no perfect setup (if there is, it doesn't repeat often enough for me), the Two-Day Rule provides sound trading guidelines. Because there are enough markets that offer plenty of trading opportunities, you can afford to be choosy. With study and experience, you will learn how the many imperfect pattern setups behave. Now let's see the Two-Day Rule in action.

March Eurocurrency

In Figure 3.10, the March Eurocurrency rallies for nine days without even a minimum price correction. It finally peaks at .8954 on December 6 (B). The two days following the high close both close lower than they opened. You now have identified a possible swing trade that meets the criteria of the Two-Day Rule.

After the markets close, you perform your calculations to determine the trigger price to enter the trade. This will allow you to be prepared for the next trading day. As the experts say, "Have your plan ready and then trade the plan." *You can wait until the trigger price is hit before calculating the target price and trade duration.*

March Eurocurrency trades higher the next day but never reaches the trigger price. You therefore recalculate the trigger price for the following day (to be ready when the market opens). This process continues each day until the fourth day when the Eurocurrency hits a low of .8751—this becomes the lowest closing price of this Reaction swing (C). The following day, the market takes a quick turn and trades sharply higher to hit the trigger price of .8849.

Once filled at .8849 (the trigger price), a protective stop is placed under the low at C. Now you go through the process of finding the target price and time duration of this trade. The price range from the high (B) to

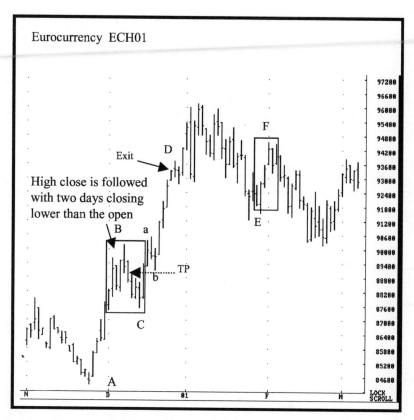

FIGURE 3.10 Swing Trades—March Eurocurrency in Uptrend

1. The Eurocurrency peaks at B. The following two days both close lower than the opening. From the low at C, the market moves through the trigger price of .8849. A strong rally follows that allows an exit of the long position at the target price of .9276 on the eighth day after the low at C.

2. Another small swing trade forms inside the larger swing trade (a to b). You could enter this small swing trade if you missed the first one. (Note: This one also meets the criteria of the Two-Day Rule.)

the previous low (A) equals .0525 points. Add .0525 points to the low of .8751 (C), to get a projected target price of .9276 (D). The time duration of this trade is eight days (a reverse count from B to A equals eight days; the forward count of eight days from C takes you to D). If the target price is not reached by the eighth trading day, you exit at the close. The target price is reached on the eighth day and the trade is closed out at .9276—a gain of .0427 points.

The March Eurocurrency continues the upward trend until January 5, when it peaks at .9615 and then turns lower. Three weeks into the new downward trend, the Eurocurrency spends one week in a correction. This forms a new Reaction swing, marked as E to F in Figure 3.11. The first two days of the correction both have closing prices above their opening prices; this meets the criteria of the Two-Day Rule. The market correction continues for one more day before it reverses to resume the original downward trend.

The trigger price to enter the short position sits at .9320. When this price is hit a new swing trade is confirmed. The target price is calculated as .9020. The reverse count (from E to the high at 15) stipulates that the trade will last no longer than 15 days projected from the high pivot at F. On day 15, the trade hits the target price of .9020.

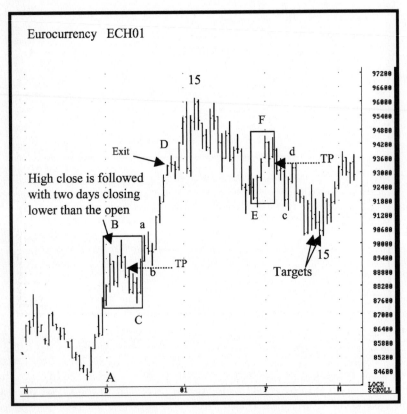

FIGURE 3.11 Swing Trade—Eurocurrency in Downtrend Market

Another small swing trade occurs at c to d that hits its target price. (Note: This also fits the Two-Day Rule.)

March Treasury Bonds

In Figure 3.12, the March T-Bonds are in a well-established upward trend when a Reaction swing begins to form on November 30 (B). The following two days meet the criteria for the Two-Day Rule. After the sec-

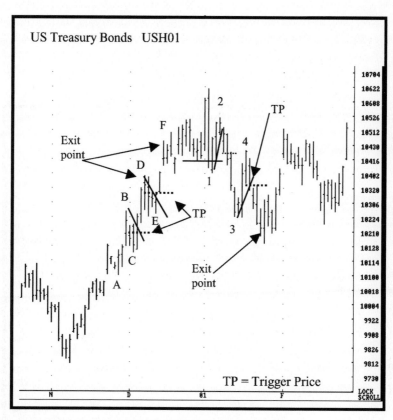

FIGURE 3.12 Swing Trading—U.S. Treasury Bonds Market

1. The first two swing trades—B to C and D to E—both reach the target price within the time permitted.

2. A new rising Reaction swing forms from 1 to 2. A new sell swing trade could be initiated in which the trigger price is hit for a successful short trade. This also signals the end of the bull market and the beginning of the bear market.

3. The next swing trade of 3 to 4 is also successful.

ond down day close, the trigger price should be calculated—it is 102-09. The reverse count to the low at A projected forward indicates the duration of the trade is no longer than three days. The target price (price range from B to A, projected forward from C) of 103-20 is hit on the third day of the trade and the market goes immediately into another Reaction swing. A new trigger price, target, and time duration are all calculated. The trigger price of 103-12 is hit and the target price at 105-02 is reached on the third trade day. If the target price had not been reached on the third day, the trade would have been exited at the close of the third day.

Now look at the Reaction swing marked 1 to 2. It is a rising Reaction swing after a big one-day price drop (a drop that confirmed a series of days of lower lows). A short swing trade could be entered at this Reaction swing. Calculate the trigger price and place it in the market. The trigger price would be filled to confirm a sell. This is the end of a bullish trend. The market is now making lower highs and lower lows. As soon as the T-Bonds trade below the previous low, the momentum kicks in for the bears. Another short trading opportunity occurs two weeks into the new downtrend when a Reaction swing forms from 3 to 4.

SWING TRADING WITH INTRADAY CHARTS

For some traders, holding a position for 5 to 10 days is an eternity. For these traders there are intraday charts. The same principles of swing trading apply, but on a shorter-term basis. The next examples demonstrate swing trading on a 30-minute chart of the June Dow Jones contract (Figure 3.13). During a three-day time span, the 30-minute chart offers four short-term swing trading opportunities.

June Dow Jones

On April 17, the June Dow Jones futures contract establishes a high at 10,335 before trading lower for the remainder of the day. Midway through this trading session, the Dow stages a one-hour rally. This rally is enough to set up the first potential swing trade (1), using the Two-Day Rule, or in this case, the Two-Bar Rule. The Dow hits the trigger price of 10,260 to enter the short position. The target price is calculated to be 10,205 and the time duration to be 90 minutes (three price bars). The Dow Jones reaches the target price on the third bar to close the short position at 10,205. This price bar also marks the beginning of a new Reaction swing.

Short covering causes the Dow Jones to rally into the close. This rally

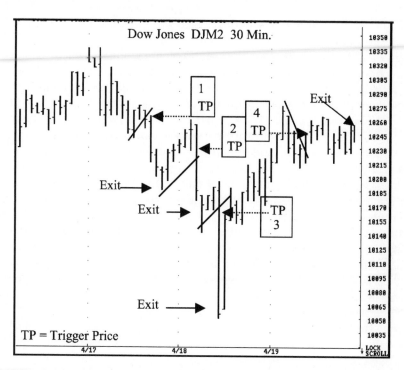

FIGURE 3.13 Swing Trading—30-Minute Chart

1. Swing trades 1 through 3 are all closed out at the target price.

2. After hitting the trigger price, swing trade 4 fails to make a new high or low. For the entire duration of the trade, the market stays within the high and low of the Reaction swing. The long position is finally closed on the last day permitted by the swing trade rules.

continues throughout the first hour of the next trading day, April 18. But within the next 30 minutes, the Dow reverses and drops through the trigger price at 10,223. This confirms another short position (2). The target price of 10,169 is reached before the time duration target. During the next hour of trading, a third Reaction swing forms.

After closing higher than the open for two consecutive price bars, the market quickly drops. The trigger price (3) for the new short position is 10,165. The target price for this trade is 10,076. Both the entry price and target price for this trade (3) are hit during the same 30-minute time period.

This trade illustrates the need to move quickly when trading in a shorter time frame. The Dow encounters massive selling immediately after the short position is entered. The market reaches the target price of 10,111 within a matter of minutes. In this particular case, the market continues past the target price and offers plenty of opportunities to exit the trade. However, this is not always the case. If you are going to trade in a shorter time frame, be ready to implement your trading plan quickly and to stick to it. As you can see in this chart example, the market rebounded quickly to erase almost all of the loss by the end of the trading day.

The last swing trade (4) illustrates another very important swing trading principle. When a bullish trend is near exhaustion, it will no longer continue to make new higher highs and higher lows. In this example, as soon as the momentum begins to shift from bullish to bearish, the market fails to make a new high. After this failure, the Dow retests the previous low and then attempts a second rally. However, the second rally also fails to trade above the previous high. This is a strong warning sign of changing market sentiment. This particular trade runs out of time and the trade is closed before the market makes a pivot and trades lower. The duration of this trade is 11 bars. The 11th bar occurs on the high bar of the second attempt. The long position is closed out at 10,252—slightly above the entry price of 10,244.

Swing trading success depends on the strength or weakness of a market, as well as how well the trading plan is followed. The best trading opportunities generally appear early in a market trend. As the trend nears exhaustion, the odds for success decrease. At the end of a long-term trend, market momentum can disappear quickly. Sometimes the market will even turn quickly and dramatically against you. This can leave many inexperienced traders with the feeling they have just been ambushed by the markets. Even though this change in market momentum seems sudden and without warning, there are usually warning signs that hint of a pending market direction change before it actually happens.

Unfortunately, after a period of good luck, some traders may begin to violate their trading plans and their personal risk management rules. These traders begin to chase dangerous positions even when the red flags are waving a warning. This leaves them unprepared and vulnerable when the market shifts momentum.

There are many warning signs that foreshadow trend exhaustion. These include: the end of a natural market cycle in a predetermined sequence, price patterns that foretell possible trend exhaustion, and momentum indicators that portend a shift in market strength or weakness. These are all tools used by successful traders. The following chapters in this book describe, illustrate, and explain in detail these and many more important characteristics of market behavior.

CHAPTER 4

The Reaction Cycle

The Reaction swing is a tremendous timing tool that can be very useful in determining the duration of a market move. This is helpful when trying to decide when to enter or exit the market. However, it gets even better when you learn about the Reaction cycle. Knowledge of the Reaction cycle will help you to determine if the market is just beginning a major market move, where the center of the move should occur, and where and when this market move should end. Yes, identifiable cycles occur in the market. Once they have been identified, you can predict (with fairly accurate results) just how the market will unfold.

BEGINNING OF THE REACTION CYCLE

The beginning of the Reaction cycle occurs at the end of a significant move in the market—in other words, at a major top or bottom. You will be looking for a market that has just made a new intermediate-term high/low. This new high or low should occur after a Reaction swing, with the price trading at or above the high or at or below the low of the Reaction swing. For example, *in an uptrend* the market should trade at or above the previous high made by the Reaction swing. *In a downtrend* the market should trade at or below the low of the previous Reaction swing.

When the market makes this new high/low and then fails to follow through, a price reversal typically will follow. This reversal is possibly the beginning of a new Reaction cycle and a new trend in the market.

If this is the beginning of a new Reaction cycle, a new trend will soon begin in the market. Once the new trend has started, wait for the market to form the first Reaction swing. This is the measuring point where it all begins.

Now that I have you thoroughly confused, let's look at some examples of markets forming these patterns just discussed. Hopefully, what you have just read will start to make some sense. I am a big believer in the old saying, "A picture is worth a thousand words." Therefore, I will use a lot of charts to illustrate what I am saying because good traders don't necessarily make good writers. Therefore, the more pictures the better.

We will follow three markets through the entire Reaction cycle, showing you step-by-step how to identify the beginning, the center, and the end of the entire cycle.

Many times, the contract high/low will occur on a projected Reversal date. This offers a great opportunity to establish a new position at the beginning of a new market trend. However, picking the top or bottom can be risky, so be sure to use a protective stop. The best way to enter the market in this type of situation is to enter a buy stop above the high of the Reversal date (if it is a new low) or just below the low of the Reversal date (if it is a new high). Keep the order working for three days. If it is not filled in these three days, cancel the order and wait for the next Reversal date.

FIRST REACTION SWING

Once the market establishes a new contract low, it is ready to trade higher. The market will usually trade up to the first resistance area. Normally, this is near the last Reaction swing in the downtrend. At this area, the market will retrace and begin to form a new Reaction swing. This new Reaction swing is the first of the new uptrend and is of vital importance in projecting the next move in the market. Some of you will recognize this pattern as a head and shoulders bottom. It can also be called a W bottom or a 1-2-3 bottom.

Once the Reaction swing is formed, the first thing to do is perform the reverse count. As we have learned, this is done by counting backward from the beginning of the new Reaction swing.

Start the reverse count at the highest close of the new Reaction swing. From this point, count backward to the beginning of the previous Reaction swing. Since the market just made a new contract low, the count will continue past the low to the low of the last Reaction swing. Remember, in a downward trending market, the beginning of a Reaction swing is the lowest close; in an upward trending market, the beginning of the Reaction swing will be the highest close.

In Figure 4.1, the first low close in Live Cattle is marked as A. From here the market trades sideways to higher before trading lower and posting a new low close, marked B.

From the low close at B, the Cattle rally for four days before closing on its high at C. This is the beginning of the first Reaction swing. Five days after the high close at C, the Cattle post a low close at D and then trade higher to continue the new uptrend. This completes the Reaction swing and confirms the beginning of the new Reaction cycle.

You now can use this information to project how far the market

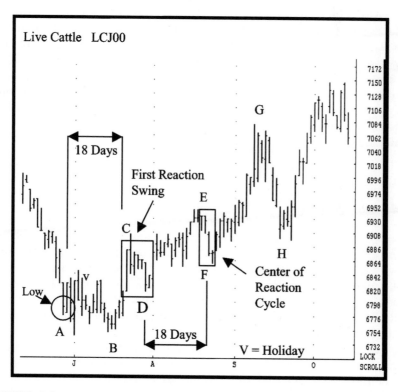

FIGURE 4.1 Reaction Cycle

1. The first Reaction swing occurs from July 22 (C) to July 29 (D).

2. The reverse count from C to A equals 18 days. The forward count of 18 days from D takes you to F.

3. The Reaction swing at E to F is the *Center of the Reaction cycle.*

should move and how long it will take for the market to move to that price level. Let's continue with the Live Cattle example.

Once the Reaction swing is identified, you perform the reverse count. Remember to start the count on the first bar to the left of the high close (C). The count continues all the way back to the lowest close at A. This means you can count past the low close at B to the low close at A. This count will help you project where the center of the Reaction cycle should occur. The reverse count back to B will usually predict only a small correction in the market. The true center of the cycle is determined by projecting forward the same number of days that were counted in the reverse count from C to A.

Let's see how this works on the Live Cattle chart, Figure 4.1. The reverse count from C to A is 18 days. Remember to count one day for the holiday in July.

Now, complete the forward count. Remember, this starts on the first bar to the right of the lowest close of the Reaction swing. This is marked as D on the chart. Count forward 18 days (this number is the same as the reverse count). This brings you to another low close at the end of another Reaction swing, marked as E to F in Figure 4.1. *This Reaction swing, formed by E to F, is the center of the Reaction cycle.* The fact that the projected reversal date is at the end of this Reaction swing tells you the market is ready to make another leg higher. It is a good time to be long the Cattle.

CENTER OF THE REACTION CYCLE

Now that you have established the Reaction swing of E to F as the center of the Reaction cycle, you can project how far the market should move from this point and how long it will take for the market to reach this objective. You always use this same method to find the center of the Reaction cycle. The forward count will usually predict the Reversal day to be the high or the low of this Reaction swing. However, I have seen times when the Reversal day falls within the Reaction swing. When this occurs, the Reversal date will usually be the center of the Reaction swing. If the Reversal date falls one or two days before or after the Reaction swing, you can still use this Reaction swing as the center of the cycle.

Now that you have successfully identified the center of the Reaction cycle, it is time to take the next step and project the end of the cycle. This is done by doing another reverse count starting at the beginning of the Reaction swing that marks the center of the cycle, in this example E and F. You then count back to the lows at D, B, and A and to the high at C (see Figure 4.2).

Starting at E, the reverse count back to D equals 15 days, to C 20 days, to B 24 days, and to A 38 days. Next, using these totals, begin the forward count from the end of this Reaction swing, marked F.

What happens in the market from this point on is very interesting. The second half of the cycle seems to be a reflection of the first half of the cycle. (Not all markets are as nicely laid out as this example, but they do follow a similar sequence.)

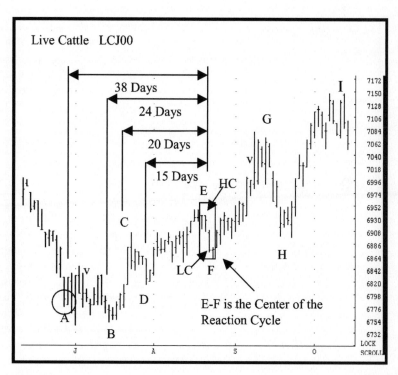

FIGURE 4.2   Reaction Cycle—First Half

1. The Reaction swing (E to F) has been identified as center of the Reaction cycle.

2. The reverse count back to D is 15 days, to C is 20 days, to B is 24 days, and to A is 38 days.

FORWARD COUNT

The forward count of 15 days from the low at F takes you to a high at G, as shown in Figure 4.3. The count of 20 days finds you at the low at H.

This is where it gets really interesting. The reverse count to the low at B is 24 days and to the low at A is 38 days. These two numbers are very important because one of them will identify the end of the cycle and usually the end of the trend. The first number to check is the low at B that gave a reverse count of 24 days. Completing the forward count, 24 days comes just as the market trades higher from the low at H. Since a reversal pattern is not confirmed, the market should continue higher into the next projected Reversal date that is due to occur on day 38. The market does trade higher into the predicted Reversal date (I) and, right on schedule, the Cat-

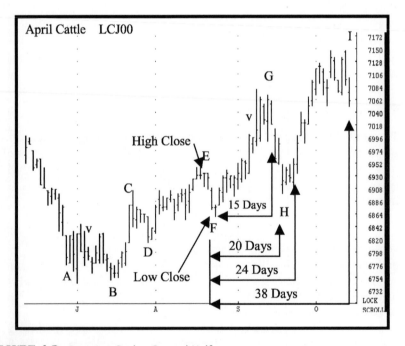

FIGURE 4.3   Reaction Cycle—Second Half

1. The center of the Reaction cycle is identified at E to F.

2. The forward count of 15 days projects a high at G. The forward count of 20 days projects a low at H.

3. The forward count of 24 days proves to be a continuation pattern. *The market never trades below the low of the Reversal day.*

4. The forward count of 38 days marks the end of the trend at I.

tle tops and trades sharply lower. This Reaction cycle is complete, and the market is ready to begin a new Reaction cycle.

As mentioned earlier, the lows at A and B are used to project the end of the cycle. If the market from point B does not give a confirming pattern, the market should trade to the Reversal date from A before ending the cycle. If you are already in the market, or even if you are looking to enter the market and catch the reversal, a good way to use this is to monitor the projected Reversal date. In this case, the Reversal date projected from the low at B trades on the 24th day above the high of the previous day. This marks the beginning of a possible reversal. Now place a sell stop under the low of this day. If the market does reverse at this point, your long position will be closed or you will be filled in a short position at the beginning of a new cycle.

In this example, the market continues higher. The trader who is already long could remain in the position with confidence that the market should continue higher for 14 more days. On the 38th day (I) when the next Reversal date is due, the trader can either exit the long position near the high of the cycle or move the protective stop up to just below the low of the Reversal date. Either way, the trader is out of the position with profit as soon as the market reverses.

Treasury Bonds

The next chart, Figure 4.4, is a good example of the complete Reaction cycle in the T-Bonds. The first thing you want to locate is the beginning of the new cycle (it is also the end of another Reaction cycle). You can find it in early December, marked B on the chart. The small Reaction swing A is an important clue that the T-Bonds are about to top.

From the high at B, the T-Bonds drop into the low at C and rally to a high at D. This forms the first Reaction swing. Now it is time to do a reverse count and then use this number to project the next Reversal date and also find the center of the cycle.

A reverse count from the beginning of the Reaction swing (C) to the high of the last Reaction swing (A) comes to 20 days. Now count forward 20 days from the end of the Reaction swing (D). You identify a date (E) in late January as the projected Reversal date. This date happens to be the exact low before a two-week rally takes the T-Bonds from 109-00 to over 113-00. You also have just identified the beginning of the Reaction swing that will be the center of the Reaction cycle.

Now you are probably saying, "Wow, this is great, but the market rallied for two weeks. How do you know when this Reaction swing will top?" That's a fair question. Look at Figure 4.5 and you will see that the market is in a minor upward trend. Six days into the rally, the T-Bonds

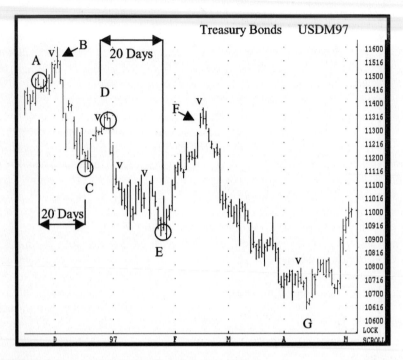

FIGURE 4.4 Reaction Cycle—First Reaction Swing

1. The T-Bonds make a major high on December 3 (B).

2. On December 18 the low close at C marks the beginning of a Reaction swing that ends on December 27 at D.

3. The Reverse count from C back to A equals 20 days. The forward count of 20 days from D projects a Reversal date of January 27 (E).

4. The projected Reversal date of January 27 (E) has a closing price of 109-09. This is the lowest close before a rally up to 113-14.

form a small Reaction swing marked 1 to 2. Using this Reaction swing to project forward, you can calculate a Reversal date due at F—this does prove to be the high. (Counting backward from 1 to the low at E equals six days. Counting forward six days from 2 takes you to the high at F.) All you need to do now is to place a sell stop under the low of the Reversal day at F and wait for the reversal to happen. When the order is filled, you will now be short the T-Bonds at the beginning of this major downward move.

Another way to confirm the Reaction swing is to draw a trend line along the lows of the two-week rally. When the market has two closes below the trend line, the Reaction swing is complete.

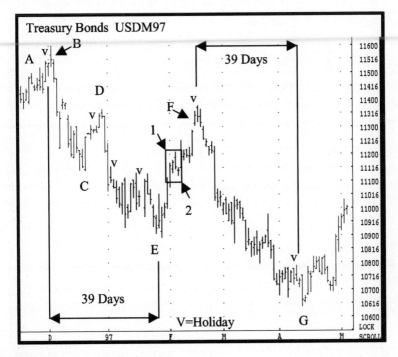

FIGURE 4.5 Reaction Cycle—Center

1. A small Reaction swing begins on February 4 (1) and ends on February 6 (2). This projects F as a Reversal date.

2. The Reaction swing of E to F is identified as the center of the Reaction cycle.

3. The reverse count from E back to B equals 39 days. The forward count of 39 days from F projects a Reversal date for April 11 (G).

4. On April 11, the T-Bonds close at 106-20 (G). This proves to be the lowest closing price before a reversal occurs.

You have now identified the Reaction swing of E to F as the center of the Reaction cycle. With this information you can now accurately project the time duration and price distance that the T-Bonds should travel before the cycle is complete.

Starting at the low of the Reaction swing (E), count backward to the beginning of the Reaction cycle—the high close at B. This count equals 39 days.

Since this is the center of the Reaction cycle, the market should continue lower for 39 days to complete the end of the cycle. This example shows you that the market bottomed exactly 39 days (G) from the end of the Reaction swing (F). Of course, you already knew this would happen!

March Cotton

Let's look at one more example of the Reaction cycle. This time we'll use a chart of March Cotton (see Figure 4.6). As you can see, the market tops out in mid-October at B, then begins to trade lower. This is the beginning of the cycle. Six days later, the Cotton has a low close (C) and then trades against the new downtrend. The high close at D forms the first Reaction swing of C to D.

Now perform the reverse count from the low close at C back to the high of the previous Reaction swing, marked A. *Remember the reverse count from the first Reaction swing always goes back to the high of the Reaction swing that occurred just before the market established a major high. The opposite is true if the market just established a major low.* This reverse count equals 16 days.

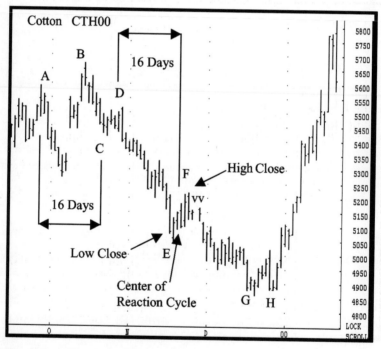

FIGURE 4.6   Reaction Cycle—Beginning

1. The first Reaction swing is identified at C and D.

2. The reverse count from C back to A equals 16 days. The forward count of 16 days projects a Reversal date of November 18.

3. The Reversal date of November 18 falls in the exact center of the Reaction swing of E to F. This marks the exact center of the Reaction cycle.

Now for the forward count. Starting with the high close at D, count forward 16 days. The 16th day falls right in the center of the Reaction swing of E to F. This Reaction swing is the center of the Reaction cycle. The low close (E) that started the Reaction swing occurred two days before the projected Reversal date, and the high close (F) that ended the Reaction swing occurred two days after the projected Reversal date. Therefore, this 16th day close is the *exact* center of the Reaction cycle.

Now that the center of the Reaction cycle has been identified, the reverse count from this Reaction swing (E to F) should tell you how many days the cycle should continue into the future. *With this information, you will know how far and how long the trend should continue.* As shown in Figure 4.7, a reverse count from the low close at E to the low

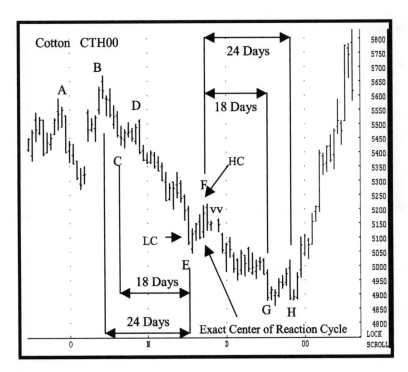

FIGURE 4.7 Reaction Cycle—Center

1. The reverse count from E back to the low close at C equals 18 days. The reverse count to B equals 24 days.

2. The forward count of 18 days and 24 days from the high close at F projects a Reversal date to fall on December 16 (G) and December 24 (H).

3. Remember to count the holidays marked with a V.

close at C equals 18 days. Continue the count back to the high close at B and you get 24 days.

Counting forward the 18 days and 24 days from the high close at F has the market making lows at G and H—the double bottom that occurs just before a strong reversal rally. You just can't get much better than that!

A DIFFERENT ENDING

The final price move in a trend can sometimes be identified by a different forward count from the final Reaction swing. This type of forward count is generated from a reverse count that goes back only to the ending period of the prior Reaction swing rather than to the beginning period as in other reverse counts. This means that the reverse count would end at the high of the Reaction swing in a downtrending market and at the low of the Reaction swing in an uptrending market.

This counting deviation applies only to an ending move, and it does not occur often.

CHAPTER 5

Reaction Lines

In the 1920s, Roger Babson wrote about how the physical law of action and reaction is reflected in economic movements. Babson, who wrote several books on business and finance, was regarded as an authority on the application of Sir Isaac Newton's law of action and reaction as it relates to business and stock market price swings. In 1928 and 1929, he was probably one of the most vocal experts warning that the great bull market was soon going to end with an equally great crash. However, like people today, no one believed that the good times would ever end. He simply stated that economic phenomena move up and down. In other words, economic activity will not go in one direction without a movement in the opposite direction.

In the early 1960s, one of Babson's close friends and students, Dr. Alan Andrews, began to provide a study course based on the theory of the law of action and reaction. One of the techniques that he taught was called the "Median Line Study." This technique employed a set of chart lines that were drawn from a significant low or high through the center of the following Reaction swing. Lines were drawn that were parallel to the center line from the high and low of the Reaction swing. When completed, these three lines resembled a pitchfork. Eventually, the set of lines became known as the "Andrews pitchfork," and it can be found on many charting programs.

I have found that the combination of Roger Babson's action/reaction theory and Dr. Alan Andrews' pitchfork is a powerful indicator of future price action. It seems that I have combined the two in a rather unusual way; yet it has proved to be an uncanny combination for price projection. The following examples demonstrate this point.

ACTION/REACTION LINES

Action/Reaction lines are drawn from the highest closing price to the lowest closing price of an existing Reaction swing. The first line is called the Action line and is used to determine the slope of the future Reaction line. Once both lines are in place I can calculate future price projections and levels where new Reaction swings will most likely occur. Let me show you how they work in some examples.

Live Cattle

The first step is to locate and draw an Action line, as illustrated in Figure 5.1. This is done at the first Reaction swing. I simply draw a straight line from the high of the Reaction swing to the low of the Reaction swing. This is called the Action line.

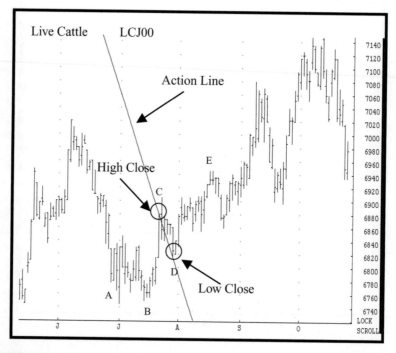

FIGURE 5.1 Action Line
1. Find the highest closing price of the Reaction swing.
2. Find the lowest closing price of the Reaction swing.
3. Draw a line from the high to the low. This is the Action line.

Once you have drawn the Action line, you need to locate the center of the Reaction cycle (this is done by calculating the center of the Reaction swing). As shown in Figure 5.2, do this by subtracting the lowest price of the Reaction swing (D) from the highest price (C). In this example, the high price is 68.80 and the low price is 68.15. Subtract 68.15 from 68.80 and you get .65 points. Now divide .65 by 2. This equals .325; round it to .33 Subtract .33 from the high price of 68.80 to equal 68.47. This price, 68.47, is the center of the Reaction swing.

On the Action line you have previously drawn, mark the center of the Reaction swing using the number just calculated (68.47).

Now draw a line from the low at B through the exact center of the Reaction swing of C to D and continue the line forward to the end of the chart. This center line has just divided the market in the exact center.

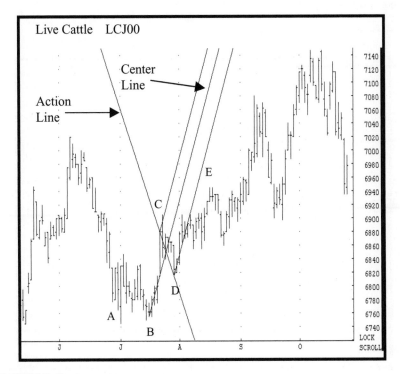

FIGURE 5.2 Center Line

1. Find the exact center of the Reaction swing of C to D by subtracting the low price from the high price and dividing by 2. Add the result to the low or subtract it from the high. Mark this price on the Action line.

2. Draw a line from the low at B up through the mark on the Action line at the center of the Reaction swing of C to D. This is the center line.

This will identify the Action and the Reaction. The first half, from B to the center of C to D, is the Action, and the last half, from the center of E to F, is the Reaction.

If this is indeed the exact center, you should be able to measure the *Action price* to project the *Reaction price*. I will show you how this is done.

Do a reverse count from the high of the Reaction swing marked C to D in Figure 5.3. From C, count back to the low close at A. (Unlike the reverse count to project time when you include holidays, do not include holidays in the reverse count to project price.) The reverse count comes to 17 bars. The next step is to do the forward count from the low of the Reaction

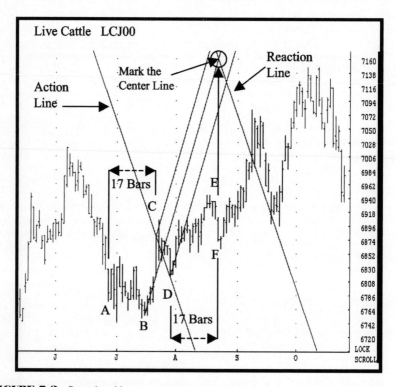

FIGURE 5.3 Reaction Line

1. Do a reverse count from the high of the first Reaction swing at C to the low at A. This count equals 17 bars. When projecting the price with Action/Reaction lines you will count only the price bars and *do not* include holidays.

2. Count forward 17 bars from the low at D and mark this on the center line. This mark is circled on this example.

3. At the circle, draw a line parallel to the first Action line drawn from C to D. This is the Reaction line.

swing. Starting at D, count forward 17 bars and mark it on the center line. Next, draw a line from this mark on the center line exactly parallel to the first Action line drawn through the Reaction swing of C to D. This is called a Reaction line. See what happens? The market forms another Reaction swing, directly on the line.

When the market breaks out of the Reaction swing at C and D, it should continue to trade along the center line and up to this new Reaction line before any correction in the market should occur. This Reaction line is your target price. As you can see, this works in conjunction with the Reversal date.

Some charting software includes the Andrews pitchfork. The software will calculate the exact center of the Reaction swing and draw the center line for you. Therefore, you will not use the two lines on either side of the center line.

Earlier you identified the Reaction swing of E to F as the center of the Reaction cycle by using time—in other words, projecting the date. You now have just projected the center of the Reaction swing by using price. This is where time and price come together.

Since this Reaction swing has been identified as the center of the Reaction cycle, you can now use it to project future movements in this market. To do this, you will use the Reaction swing at E to F in Figure 5.4 the same way you used the Reaction swing of C to D. Draw the Action line from the high of the Reaction swing (E) to the low of the Reaction swing (F). Now find the exact center of this Reaction swing and mark it on the line. Draw the center line from the low of the previous Reaction swing (D) through the Reaction swing of E and F. Continue this line to the end of the chart. The next thing to do is the reverse count from the high close at E back to the low close at D. This count equals 15 bars. Next, count forward the 15 bars from the low close of this Reaction swing (F) and mark this point on the center line. At this mark, draw the Reaction line parallel to the Action line drawn though the Reaction swing of E to F. As you can see from the chart example (Figure 5.4), the market traded to this Reaction line where it immediately changed direction and began a sharp correction. Once again, time and price came together, exactly where they were projected.

After the market traded to this Reaction line, it immediately began a market correction. This market correction formed yet another Reaction swing. You will recall that in Figure 4.3, the high at G and the low at H were already identified as Reversal dates. The market reversed exactly where the Reaction line predicted. Once again, time and price have come together.

In Figure 5.5, we continue the reverse count from E back to the low at B. This count equals 24 bars. Count forward 24 bars and place a mark at

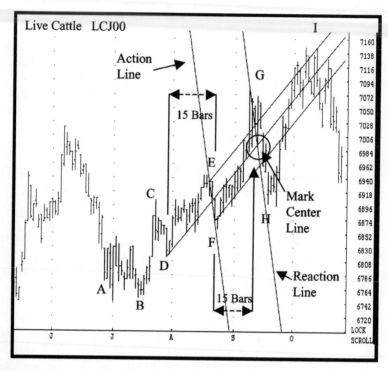

FIGURE 5.4   Action/Reaction Lines

1. The center of the Reaction cycle is the Reaction swing of E to F.

2. Draw the Action line from the high to the low of the Reaction swing.

3. Draw the center line from the low at D up and through the center of the Reaction swing. Do the reverse and forward count (15 bars) and mark the center line. Draw a Reaction line parallel to the Action line. This Reaction line projects the price where the new Reaction swing of G to H will begin.

this point on the center line. Next, draw a Reaction line parallel to the Action line through E and F. Do you notice how this example is different from the previous one? In the previous examples, a Reaction swing formed at the Reaction line. However, in Figure 5.5, the market trades right through the Reaction line after a slight pause. Remember from Figure 4.3 that the 24th bar was an unconfirmed Reversal date as the market continued to the next Reversal date. This tells you that the market is strong and it should continue trading higher into the next projected Reaction line.

The past few examples have shown you how to use a current Reaction swing to project a future Reaction swing. The next example illustrates how to use the center of the Reaction cycle to project the end of the cycle by means of price and time.

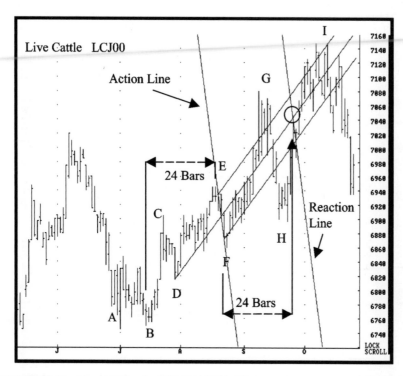

FIGURE 5.5 Action/Reaction Lines—Reversal Dates

1. The center of the Reaction cycle is identified as E to F. The Action line and the center line have been identified and drawn.

2. If you continue the reverse count back to the major low at B, you get 24 bars. The forward count projects a Reversal date on September 28 marked with a circle. The Reaction line is drawn through this date.

3. On the Reaction day, the market trades through the Reaction line. This confirms that the Cattle will continue higher into the next projected Reversal date, projected to occur on October 13 (I).

Using the center of the Reaction cycle that has been identified as the Reaction swing at E and F in Figure 5.6, draw the Action line and the center line. Next, proceed with the reverse count. This time, continue the reverse count past B and back to A. This count equals 37 bars. Following the same procedure done previously, count forward 37 days from F and mark the center line at I. Once the Reaction line is drawn, you have identified the exact high of the entire move in Cattle. Once again, this example demonstrates the power of time and price working together.

Do you notice that you are always counting back to the lows?

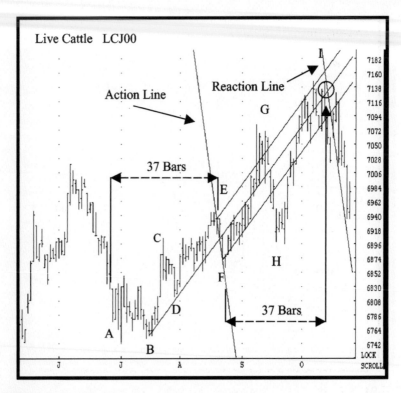

FIGURE 5.6 Action/Reaction Lines—Time and Price

1. The Reaction swing of E to F is identified as the center of the Reaction cycle. The Action line and center line have been properly located and drawn.

2. The reverse count from E back to A equals 37 bars. The forward count of 37 bars is marked on the center line at I.

3. The Cattle trade at 71.47 on the projected Reversal date of October 13. This price and date could have been predicted over one month earlier. Time and price came together perfectly!

Always count back to the lows in a downward trending market. If the market is trending higher, count back to the highs.

Treasury Bonds

We will now look at an example in the T-Bonds market (see Figure 5.7). Using the first Reaction swing of C to D, draw in the Action line and the center line. The reverse count begins at the low close at C and proceeds back to the high close at B. This count equals 11 bars. Now count forward 11 bars from the high at D and mark this on the center line. Now draw a Reaction line par-

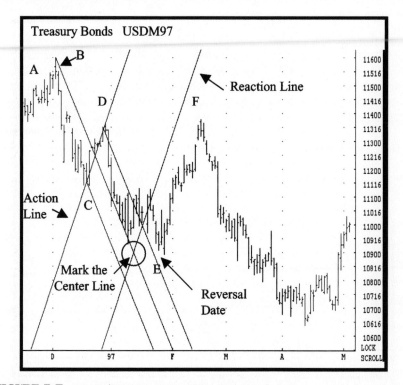

FIGURE 5.7 Action/Reaction Lines—First Reaction Swing

1. The T-Bonds make a major high on December 3 (B), closing at 115-16. The first Reaction swing then forms at C and D. Once this Reaction swing is identified, the Action line and center line are drawn.

2. The reverse count from C to B equals 11 bars. The forward count of 11 bars is marked on the center line, and the Reaction line is drawn parallel to the Action line.

3. The T-Bonds trade down to the projected price at the Reaction line. After forming a consolidation pattern, the T-Bonds drop past the Reaction line into the next Reversal date at E.

allel to the Action line drawn through C to D. As you can see, the T-Bonds trade lower into the Reaction line. Just before the Reaction line, the T-Bonds form a small consolidation pattern. Once the market trades through the Reaction line, it quickly falls right into the projected Reversal date (E). (Remember that you identified this Reversal date in Figure 4.5.) The Reaction line provides a reliable target for the market. Based on the information you've gathered using this method, you know in advance that the market is due for a correction precisely at this price level and time. You also know from previous work on the Reaction cycle that this correction is the center of the Reaction cycle and most likely the center of a much larger move. With this knowledge, you can use this new Reaction swing of E to F to project forward and identify where and when this trend and cycle will likely end. You can do this by repeating the process that you have just completed.

The T-Bonds complete the upward move at the projected Reversal date (F). The reversal is confirmed as the T-Bonds start to trade lower. Once we feel confident that the major trend is down, we can do price projections. By now you know the process (see Figure 5.8). Draw the Reaction line from E to F, calculate the center of the Reaction swing, and then draw the center line from the high at B down through the center of the Reaction swing of E to F.

Having done this, it is time to start the counting process. The reverse

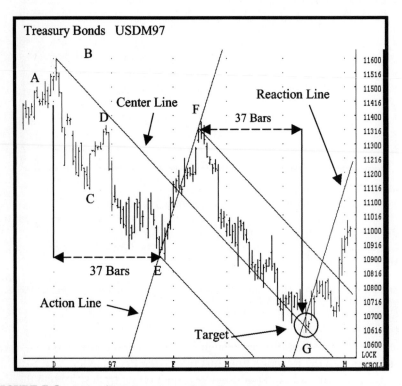

FIGURE 5.8   Action/Reaction Lines—Price Projections

1. The Reaction swing of E to F is identified as the center of the Reaction cycle. The Action line and center line are properly drawn.

2. The reverse count from E to B is 37 bars. The forward count of 37 bars is marked on the center line (G).

3. The T-Bonds trade lower to make a major low at 106-12, right on the Reaction line. This price just happens to coincide with the projected Reversal date. Once again, time and price came together.

count from E back to B equals 37 bars. Now count forward 37 bars from the high at F, mark it on the center line, and then draw the Reaction line. I think the chart speaks for itself, as time and price come together at G— right where they were projected to. This date and price could have been projected as long as six weeks before they occurred.

Cotton

Let's look at another example, this one in Cotton. The first Reaction swing is marked C and D in Figure 5.9. The Action line is drawn from the

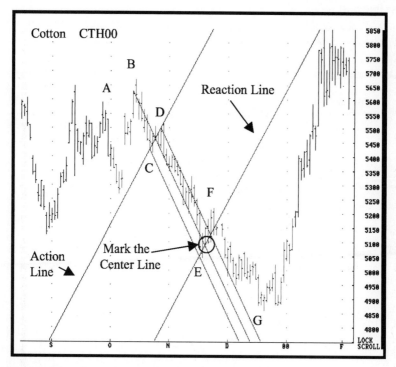

FIGURE 5.9   Reaction Line—First Reaction Swing

1. The Action line is drawn through the Reaction swing of C to D. The center of the Reaction swing of C to D is calculated, and the center line is drawn from B down and through the center of C and D to the end of the chart.

2. Based on the reverse count from C to A, the forward count is marked on the center line with a circle. The Reaction line is drawn parallel to the Action line.

3. The Cotton trades down to the price level projected by the Reaction line. The market hits the Reaction line and then forms a new Reaction swing. From Figure 4.7, you know that the bar in the exact center of this Reaction swing was a projected Reversal date. You have also just identified the center of the Reaction cycle.

low close to the high of this Reaction swing. The center of the Reaction swing is calculated, and the center line is drawn from the high at B down and through the center of the Reaction swing of C to D to the bottom of the chart.

The reverse count from the low close at C back to the high close at A equals 16 bars. The forward count of 16 bars is marked on the center line with a circle. The Reaction line is drawn parallel to the Action line. This new Reaction line is the beginning of a price correction in the market and the beginning of a new Reaction swing. You also know from previous examples that this new Reaction swing of E to F is the center of the Reaction cycle. The market did make a short-term low right on the projected Reaction line and Reversal date.

Now it's time to repeat the process from this new Reaction swing (see Figure 5.10). Draw the Action line from the low at E to the high at F. Calcu-

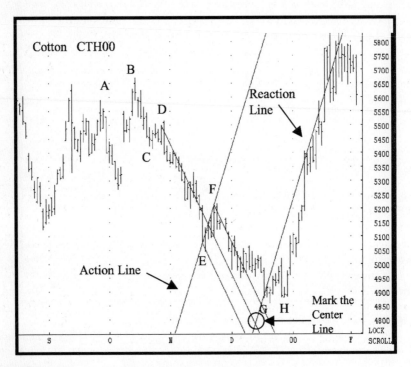

FIGURE 5.10 Reaction Line—New Reaction Swing

1. The Action line is drawn through the Reaction swing at E to F.

2. The Reaction line is drawn parallel to the Action line at the mark on the center line (this is at the price level of 48.00).

3. The Cotton trades down to the Reaction line where it reverses to confirm a major bottom.

late the center of this Reaction swing and then draw the center line from the high close at D down through the center of the Reaction swing of E to F. Next, count back from the low close at E to the high close at D. This equals 14 bars. Now count forward 14 bars from the high close at F and mark it on the center line with a circle. Next, draw the Reaction line parallel to the Action line drawn at E to F. Once again, you can see how time and price come together to reverse the market at the precise point and date (G) predicted several days earlier.

Now you are probably saying to yourself, "Wait a minute, why didn't he go all the way back to B like he has in previous examples?"

The market usually trades in three equal legs of time. I've shown you this in previous examples when we used one leg to project the time and price of the next leg. This method can be used on a long- or short-term basis. In Figure 5.10, the market makes a low at G as predicted. The Cotton trades higher off this Reaction line and is followed by a price decline into the next Reversal date at H. Here the market does not trade below the previous low. The previous low holds and the market trades higher. Because it turns higher, you can be fairly confident that the bottom has been established and the market has reversed. Therefore, it becomes unnecessary to continue the projection out from the high at B.

WHEN THE TREND DOES NOT END

So often, as soon as you get something figured out and begin to depend on it, life throws you a curveball. It is the same with the Reaction cycle: Unfortunately, there are times when the market trend does not end exactly on the last Reaction line. However, don't despair, as there are a couple of ways to handle this type of situation, and both work equally well.

If the market trades through a Reaction line that was supposed to end the cycle, simply extend the reverse count to the next Reaction swing and project forward on the same center line. Then draw a new Reaction line. The market will usually continue to this new line before reversing. Figure 5.11 in the Wheat better illustrates what I'm saying.

In Figure 5.11, the Reaction cycle is due to end at the first Reaction line. The Wheat does stop there for a few days before dropping through this Reaction line. Once the Wheat closes below this Reaction line, a trend continuation is indicated that should take the market lower into the next Reaction line. This new Reaction line is found by extending the reverse count to the previous Reaction swing and projecting it forward on the center line. The Wheat trades through the second Reaction line before

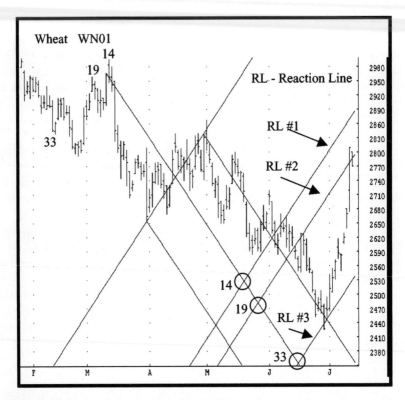

FIGURE 5.11   Extending the Reaction Cycle

1. In this example, the first and second Reaction lines are determined by the reverse counts of 14 bars and 19 bars, counted forward.

2. Extending the reverse count to the previous Reaction swing equals 33 bars. The forward count of 33 bars is marked on the center line where a third Reaction line is drawn. The Wheat trades to the third Reaction line and then reverses into a strong rally.

it reverses at the third Reaction line (use the same process to establish the third Reaction line).

This next example illustrates what happens if the new Reaction swing is used to project a new Reaction line.

Using the same chart of July wheat, let's move down to a new Reaction swing identified as A to B in Figure 5.12. This new Reaction swing can be used to project a new Reaction line.

The Action line is drawn; the reverse count equals 19 bars. This, in turn, projects a Reaction line 19 bars forward. Once the forward count is completed and the center line is marked, a Reaction line is drawn parallel

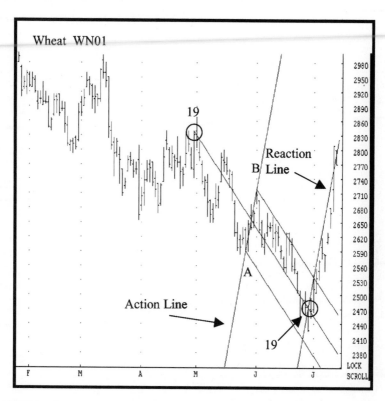

FIGURE 5.12 Extending the Reaction Cycle Using a New Reaction Swing
1. A new Reaction swing is marked A to B.
2. The reverse count from A to the high of the previous Reaction swing equals 19 bars.
3. The new Reaction line is marked on the center line, 19 bars forward from B. This time, the Wheat reverses and rallies off the Reaction line.

to the Action line. As you can see in Figure 5.12, the Wheat trades right to the Reaction line and then reverses to start a strong bull rally.

Although this market situation does not occur often, I have found that once a Reaction line is broken decisively as shown in Figure 5.11, the market has shown a strong tendency to be drawn to the next Reaction line. This method is illustrated in Figure 5.11.

CHAPTER 6

The Price Is Right

You may be asking yourself, "This is great that I now see how a Reaction cycle should unfold. But how do I know when it's time to buy or sell?" Well, this is exactly what this chapter covers.

So far this book has illustrated how a natural cycle runs through the market and how time and price work in relation to this timing cycle. This chapter will talk about natural support and resistance levels. It only stands to reason that if the market follows a natural time cycle, there will be natural price levels where the market should find support and resistance.

A general observation of the markets shows that they do not trade in a straight line. There is always a struggle for control between the bears and the bulls. In this struggle, each side enjoys victories and suffers defeats.

For example, if a market makes a nice bottom formation after an extended downward move and then trades up to a price where many chart readers believe the market will run into resistance, the bearish traders will move in and sell. The bearish traders believe that the trend is still down and this correction provides a good selling opportunity.

This, in turn, pushes the market down against the new uptrend. The result is a price correction (retracement). When this new uptrending market corrects or retraces, the price will pull back to predetermined natural support levels. These price levels tend to support any market in any time frame. By using these support levels, the trader can determine the most likely price where a correction will end before trading in the direction of the new uptrend. I call these areas the buy windows or buy zones. (In a market that is trending downward, the resistance levels are known as sell windows or sell zones.)

NATURAL SUPPORT AND RESISTANCE LEVELS

The theory of natural support and resistance levels existing in the markets is not new. It has been discussed, argued over, and interpreted for years. There is no use in reinventing the wheel, but I can certainly take the theory and put it to good use by combining it with the Reversal dates.

Reaction swings are formed when the price trades against the current trend. You have just learned that this is also called a *correction* or *retracement*. In the previous chapters, I identified the beginning or end of the Reaction swing using only projected Reversal dates. By predetermining the buy and sell windows, I will also be able to project the price level at which the correction should end. Once again, I will know what can happen when time and price come together.

Much has been written about the 50 percent retracement level. This means that the market will retrace 50 percent of the original move, find support, and then resume the current trend. Although I think this is a good rule of thumb, I have found the strongest reversals and largest moves begin at lower levels.

I have seen many times when an upward trending market retraces 50 percent of the original price move, finds support, and then trades somewhat higher for a couple of days. Just as the trader begins to feel comfortable in his position, the market reverses again and trades to a new low.

From my research and experience, *I believe the strongest reversals take place between the 61.8 percent and 78 percent retracement levels*. To make this price window easier to calculate, I use 60 percent as the beginning of the window. Whenever a market enters a buy/sell window, it is time to check for a Reversal date.

Using the buy and sell windows in conjunction with the Reversal dates provides a powerful blend of time and price. When a Reversal date occurs inside a buy or sell window, a strong price move can follow.

CALCULATING BUY/SELL WINDOWS

The market enters into the buy/sell window when it has retraced 60 percent of the original move. In other words, if the prevailing trend of the market is down, the market would have to trade higher (against the trend) to enter the sell window.

Calculating the buy/sell window is a very simple and quick process—all you need is a calculator. Even though there are many charting software programs that can do this automatically, it is a good idea to know the process.

For a sell window, you take the high price of the current move and subtract from it the low price of the current move. The low is the price made just before the market began to trade higher against the prevailing downtrend. For example, if the high price is 75.00 and the low price is 65.00, the difference is 10.00. Now calculate 60 percent of 10.00. This equals 6.00.

As I am calculating the sell window, I add the 6.00 points to the low price of 65.00 to get 71.00. This means that the market will need to trade up to 71.00 before entering into the ideal sell window. Once the market has traded above 71.00, a sell signal can occur anywhere between the beginning of the sell window and the recent high (in this case 75.00).

Here is a quick review of a sell window in a downtrend:

1. Once the market establishes an intermediate low and starts to trade higher from this low, subtract the high (the high price at the beginning of the prevailing trend prior to this intermediate low) from the low. This will equal the total price range of the original move: 75.00 – 65.00 = 10.00.

2. Now multiply the range by 60 percent: 10.00 × 60% = 6.00.

3. Add this total to the low: 65.00 + 6.00 = 71.00.

4. This price (71.00) is the beginning of the sell window.

When I calculate a buy window, I follow the same process except I *subtract* the 60 percent total from the *high* price.

Once the market has entered the sell window, wait for the next predicted Reversal date. When the market is in the sell window in conjunction with a Reversal date, a major turn in the market can occur.

April Cattle

In the following example, an April Cattle chart (Figure 6.1) illustrates a sell window. The Cattle top at 81.82 (A) and then begin a new downward trending market. The market continues to trade lower until it hits an intermediate low at 76.77 (B). The low is followed by a correction against the current downward trend. A quick calculation determines that 79.80 is the beginning of the sell window.

From the low at B, the Cattle trade higher over the next eight trading days. The Cattle enter the sell window and trade to a high of 79.95. (This

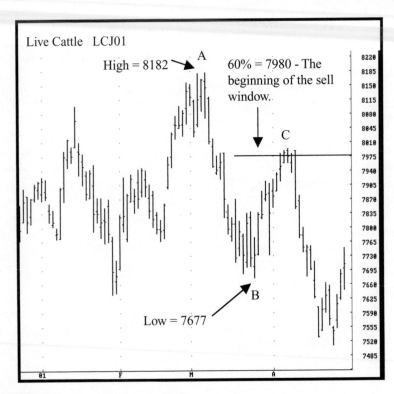

FIGURE 6.1 Buy/Sell Window (Cattle)

1. The major high is 81.82 (A) and the intermediate low price is 76.77 (B).
2. 81.82 − 76.77 = 5.05; 5.05 × 60% = 3.03; 76.77 + 3.03 = 79.80.
3. The sell window begins at 79.80.
4. The Cattle trade to just inside the sell window before resuming the downward trend.

is just .15 points inside the sell window that began at 79.80.) After poking into the sell window, the April Cattle make a quick turnaround and collapse to a new low.

Knowing in advance where a market is likely to reverse or at least run into support or resistance can help to give any trader an edge only when entering or exiting a trade.

Copper

Copper offers two good examples of a market reversing inside the buy window. In Figure 6.2 the Copper bottoms at 75.30 (A). This is followed by a nice rally up to 85.50 (B). At this point, the Copper corrects and trades

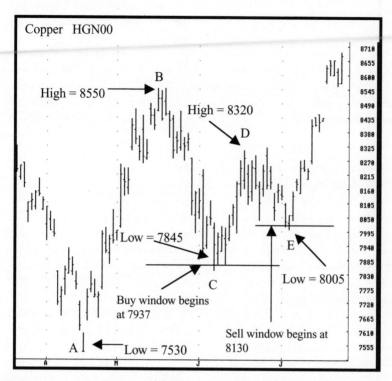

FIGURE 6.2 Buy/Sell Window (Copper)

1. The move from the low at 75.30 (A) to 85.50 (B) represents the major trend.

2. 85.50 (B) – 75.30 (A) = 10.20; 10.20 × 60% = 6.12; 85.50 – 6.12 = 79.38. The buy window is 79.38.

3. The correction ends at 78.45 (C) just inside the buy window at 79.38 and then reverses.

4. After a minor rally the Copper retraces back into another buy window at (E). The calculations are: 83.20 (D) – 78.45 (C) = 4.75; 4.75 × 60% = 2.85; 83.20 – 2.85 = 80.35. The new buy window is 80.35. After just entering the buy window, the Copper reverses to continue the upward trend.

against the current trend. A quick calculation determines that the buy window begins at 79.38. You'll see that the Copper trades to a low of 78.45 (C) (inside the buy window), before it reverses and resumes the major trend.

The resumption of the upward move in Copper is interrupted by another market correction that begins at 83.20 (D) and ends at 80.05 (E). Once again, a quick calculation determines that the buy window begins at 80.35.

The Copper trades to a low of 80.05 (E) (just inside the buy window). The correction also ends on a projected Reversal date. The combination of the 30 percent retracement and the Reversal date causes the market to quickly rally.

As you can see from these examples, the 50 percent level was violated each time and the major market reversals did not occur until the 60 percent plus retracement level. I'm not suggesting that this will happen every time, as I have seen markets turn at the 50 percent retracement. However, I believe that the 60 percent retracement offers stronger and more frequent signals.

MARKET RETRACEMENTS IN STRONGLY TRENDING MARKETS

There is always a "but" or "however" when dealing with the markets because nothing works 100 percent of the time. Using 60 percent retracements for buy and sell windows is an excellent technique for most markets. However, when the trend in a market is extremely strong, the market will usually not retrace even close to the 60 percent level. Instead, the market will begin to make small and quick corrections that usually last three to seven days. The stronger the market, the shorter the correction time period. These strongly trending markets will normally see the market retrace to around 30 percent of the original move. This level still offers some very good reversal signals. This is especially true when there is a Reversal date at the 30 percent price level as well.

The 30 Percent Retracement—March Cotton

The 30 percent retracement is very evident in the March Cotton in Figure 6.3. This is a good example of a strongly trending market. In this type of market, the corrections or retracements will not be as dramatic or as long as in most markets. This occurs because the retracements are short-lived—they last only three to seven days. For example, the price correction from C to D lasts only four days.

When I identify a strongly trending market, I never look for the large 60 percent retracement, as it rarely occurs. Instead, I always look for the 30 percent retracement because the market still has to adhere to the pattern of natural corrections.

The Cotton market gives us two excellent examples of the 30 percent retracement. The move from C to D is a retracement of the original move from the low at 54.15 (C) to the high at 56.70 (B). Let's do the calculations.

56.70 (B) − 54.15 (C) = 2.55 points
2.55 × 30% = .765 (round to .77)
54.15 + .77 = 54.92

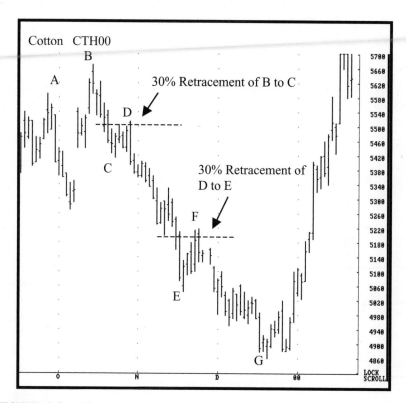

FIGURE 6.3 Sell Window—30 Percent Retracement

1. The Cotton makes a low at C and trades up to D.
2. The reversal at D occurs near the 30% retracement of the price move from B to C.
3. Cotton makes a low at E, then rallies to F.
4. The high at F occurs near the 30 percent retracement of the price move from D to E.

(Remember: In a downtrend, add the 30 percent total to the low to get the sell window.)

This minor sell window begins at 54.92. The retracement peaks at 55.15 (D) (just inside the window). As you can see in the chart example, when the Cotton trades into this minor sell window it reverses and forms an outside day that closes below the previous day's low. This price action completes the Reaction swing, and the Cotton resumes the new downward trend.

The next correction begins at 50.45 (E) and ends at 52.19 (F). This forms a new Reaction swing in the move from D 55.15 to E. The calculations are:

52.19 − 50.45 = 1.74
1.74 × 30% = .522 (round off to .52)
50.45 + .52 = 50.97

Cotton enters the minor sell window at 50.97 (F) before peaking at a high of 52.19 (F). It then reverses and trades to a new low.

The 60 Percent Retracement—April Cattle

The next example (Figure 6.4) illustrates the 60 percent retracement. On July 15, the April Cattle make a new contract low at 67.50 (B) before

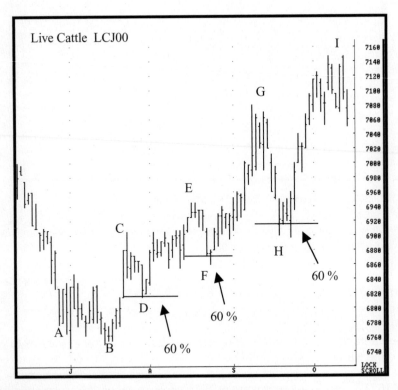

FIGURE 6.4 Buy Window—60 Percent Retracement

1. D = 60% retracement of price move from B to C. 69.05 (C) − 67.50 (B) = 1.55; 1.55 × 60% = .93; 69.05 − .93 = 68.12. The buy window is 68.12.

2. F = 60% retracement of the price move from D to E. 69.45 E − 68.15 (D) = 1.30; 1.30 × 60% = .78; 69.45 (E) − .78 = 68.67. The second buy window is 68.67.

3. H = 60% retracement of price move from F to G. 70.80 (G) − 68.60 (F) = 2.20; 2.20 × 60% = 1.32; 70.80 − 1.32 = 69.48. The third buy window is 69.48.

beginning a new bullish trend. An intermediate high is made a few days later at 69.05 (C). A quick calculation reveals that the buy window starts at 68.12. The Cattle retrace to 68.15 (D), before resuming the upward trend. You'll notice that the Cattle miss the buy window by only three points.

The next intermediate high occurs at 69.45 on August 15 (E). This is a rally of 1.30 points from the low of 68.15, marked (D) on the example chart. When you multiply 1.30 by 60 percent, the result equals .78 points. When you subtract .78 points from the high price of 69.45, you get 68.67. You know now that the buy window begins at 68.67. The Cattle trade to a low of 68.60 (F) (just inside the buy window) before reversing.

After posting the low at 68.60 (F) the Cattle rally to the next intermediate high on September 9 at 70.80 (G). This is a rally of 2.20 points from the low at 68.60 (F). Multiply 2.20 by 60 percent to get 1.32 points. Subtract 1.32 from the high of 70.80 (G) to get 69.48. Now you know that the third buy window begins at 69.48. The Cattle trade to just inside the buy window and reach a low of 68.97 on September 23 (H). As you can see from the chart example, this is an excellent place to buy the Cattle.

MORE BUY/SELL WINDOW CALCULATIONS

No market will ever trade in a straight line. The human emotions of fear and greed take effect after any sustained price move. Just before a price correction, the fear of being left behind and missing out on the anticipated profits will cause uninformed or novice traders to enter the market. Disappointment and fear of bigger losses will cause them to exit the market just as it is near the end of a correction.

Knowledge of market behavior will help you to avoid these common pitfalls that plague many traders. When you can sit back with the knowledge that the markets always fulfill their normal tendencies and with the knowledge and confidence to take advantage of these tendencies, you will become a more relaxed and more successful trader.

Buy and sell windows are just another trading tool to put in your trading toolbox. Knowing the natural tendencies of market corrections will give you that extra trading edge. When you combine this knowledge of market corrections with the knowledge of Reversal dates, the trading possibilities become phenomenal.

The next market we will go over is the T-Bonds in Figure 6.5. This will give us another opportunity to calculate a sell window. As the market is in a downward trend, the price correction will send the market higher. (This is the opposite of the previous example in Cattle.)

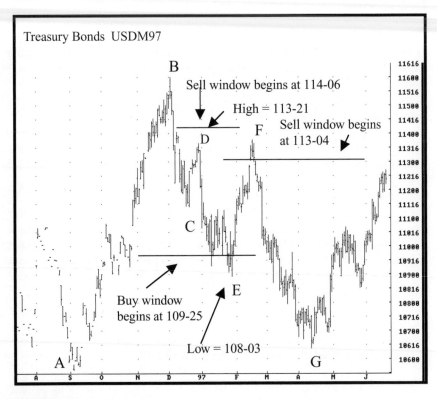

Treasury Bonds USDM97

FIGURE 6.5 Buy/Sell Window (T-Bonds)

1. 116-00 (B) − 111-14 (C) = 146; 146 × 60% = 88; 111-14 (C) + 88 = 114-06. This is the first sell window. The first market retracement ends at D falling just short of the sell window. The low of 108-30 (E) is inside the 60 percent retracement buy window of the uptrend from A to B. From the low at E, the T-Bonds rally into the sell window at 113-04 (near F).

2. The sell window, based on the price move from B to E, begins at 113-04 (near F). The T-Bonds make a significant price reversal inside this sell window.

From the high at 116-00 that occurs on December 3 (B), the T-Bonds trade down to 111-14 on December 17 (C). This is the beginning of the first Reaction swing. The difference between 116-00 and 111-14 equals 146 points. (Note: In T-Bonds, the difference between 116-00 and 115-00 is 32 points.) Multiply this amount by 60 percent to get 87.6. (Round this number to 88.) Since the T-Bonds trade in 32nds, you will need to convert the 88 points into 32nds. This converts to $2^{24}/_{32}$ (2-24).

Since we are looking for the beginning of the sell window, add the total to the low price of 111-14 (C). This equals 114-06. We have just determined that the sell window begins when the market reaches 114-06. However, the T-Bonds traded only as high as 113-21 (D), a price below the sell window, before reversing and trading lower. The price of 113-21 is actually 50 percent of the original move. This time, the T-Bonds do not reach the 60 percent level.

As previously discussed, the 50 percent retracement level is used by many traders. However, I have found many times that the market will hit the 50 percent level and break through it a few days later and then trade to the 60 percent level. I believe that the 60 percent retracement level offers better trading opportunities, especially when it is combined with Reversal dates. You may be asking yourself, "Is there any way to know if the 50 percent level will hold and work?" The next chapter shows you how you could have known that the T-Bonds had hit resistance and the 113-21 price actually offered a great selling opportunity.

The next major selling opportunity in our T-Bonds example occurs when the T-Bonds peak at 113-25 on February 18 (F). This is a retracement of the original move from the high of 116-00 (B) to the low of 108-30 (E). It is important to note that the trading day of February 18 is a projected Reversal date. This day proves to be the highest closing price before a major sell-off in the T-Bonds. As we already know there is a projected Reversal date due on February 18, we calculate the sell window to begin at 113-04.

116-00 (B) − 108-30 (E) = 7-02
(From 116-00 to 115-00 = 32)
Converted to 32nds = 224
224 × 60% = 134.4 (round to 134)
Convert to T-Bond pricing = 4-06
108-30 (E) + 4-06 = 113-04

The T-Bonds trade into the sell window and make a high 21 points above the beginning of the sell window. The high is also exactly when the projected Reversal date was predicted.

There is something else we need to look at in this example. In all the previous T-Bond examples, I have only talked about the Reaction cycle that began at the high of 116-00 (B). As you know by now, the T-Bonds traded down to 108-30 (E) before beginning a 14-day correction up to 113-25 (F). (We calculated this in the previous example.) The next question you may ask is (if you are not asking, you should), "Was the market correction of B to E a 60 percent retracement of the original trend from A to B?" The answer is yes! The market retraced into a buy window and then reversed on a projected Reversal date. Look at Figure 6.5 and do the calculations.

From the chart you can see that the bull trend began on September 5 at 105-20 (A) and ended on December 3 at 116-00 (B). Without showing all the calculations, I will just tell you that the 60 percent buy window began at 109-25. From the high at 116-00 (B), the T-Bonds traded down into the buy window and stopped at a low of 108-30 (E). The low at E just happened to be a projected Reversal date. As you can see, a sharp 13-day rally followed.

Just a quick look at the chart examples in the T-Bonds clearly demonstrates how the major buying and selling opportunities came when the T-Bonds were inside the buy/sell windows in conjunction with projected reversal timing. Why would you want to trade any other way?

CHAPTER 7

Reversal Dates and the Gann Fan

Even though there are numerous traders who are considered trading experts and gurus, only a few survive the test of time. One such trader was a man named W. D. Gann.

Before his death in 1955, Gann reportedly made as much as $50 million from trading the market—and that was when $50 million really meant something! His ability to pinpoint the exact turning points in stock and futures markets was unparalleled and legendary. For example, he predicted the 1929 stock market crash—a full nine months in advance. In 1932, he foretold that the stock market would hit a low six months before it actually did.

However, his most famous and uncanny prediction occurred in 1909. On September 21 of that year, Gann predicted that September Wheat would trade at $1.20 a bushel on or before September 30. At that time, Wheat was struggling at $1.05. When September 30 arrived (the contract expiration date), September Wheat had not moved above $1.08. In fact, it remained stagnant for much of the day.

When confronted with this apparent error, Gann stubbornly folded his arms across his chest and stated, "If it does not touch $1.20 before the market closes, it will prove that there is something wrong with my entire method of calculations. I do not care what the price is now. It must go to $1.20."

Just minutes before the contract expired, the September Wheat suddenly flew up to $1.20. Incredibly, it closed at that price!

What was W. D. Gann's response when questioned about this stunning forecast? He replied, "The future is nothing but a repetition of the past. Everything moves in cycles as a result of the natural law of action and reaction."

Gann discovered that the future is a repetition of the past based on natural order. "Everything moves in cycles as a result of the natural law of action and reaction. By studying the past I have discovered that cycles repeat in the future." The knowledge and ability to determine when one cycle ends and a new one begins offers remarkable potential. As long as human nature does not change, history will continue to repeat itself.

In Chapter 5, I referred to Andrews and Babson as past trading experts. I now want to add W. D. Gann's name to this list of great trading masters. I do not do this because I use all his information and trading techniques. (A person could spend years trying to understand all that he wrote.) Instead, I add his name to my list because most of his trading techniques are based on the theory that a natural cycle runs through the market. He was fond of saying, "The future is nothing but a repetition of the past." I understand this to mean that market cycles tend to repeat themselves and they seek out natural price levels. Of course, I like this idea because it just confirms what I have been talking about in this book.

GANN FAN

Using the theory of time and price, Gann believed that the market will seek out natural support and resistance price levels. To identify these price levels, he developed a technique to project where these levels should occur. This technique consisted of a series of lines drawn from a major low or high across a chart at different angles. Because of its resemblance to a fan, it soon became known as the "Gann fan." The series of lines in the fan are known as "Gann lines."

WHAT IS IN A FAN

The Gann fan originates from a major high or low. It consists of seven lines drawn at different angles across the chart. The center line, known as the 1×1, is drawn at a 45-degree angle—it is the most significant line. Prices tend to gravitate to the center line (1×1) while the other lines provide support and resistance.

The 1×1 line is generally used as a trend indicator. A market that is trading below the 1×1 line is considered weak; and a market trading above the 1×1 is considered a strong market. This book will not talk about the detailed trading strategies usually associated with the Gann fan. Instead, it will concentrate on how I use the Gann fan in conjunction with the Reversal dates.

Frequently, I use the Gann fan in combination with the Reversal dates and the buy/sell windows. Since the fan helps to identify natural support and resistance levels, the market tends to be drawn to these lines at the same time a reversal is due. Therefore, the Gann fan offers another tool to help confirm time and price.

When a market enters into a buy or sell window, I often rely on a Gann line to help determine a more specific entry price. A buy or sell window can help identify a price area where the market should reverse, but a Gann line will help identify a more specific price within the window. In addition, this can help to identify a more specific target price.

The following examples illustrate what I mean.

MARKING THE BEGINNING OF THE GANN FAN

The placement of the Gann fan is important and fortunately, fairly easy to do. For example, if the market is trending lower, the beginning of the Gann fan is located on the high at the beginning of the downtrend. From this high, the lines are sloped downward at different angles. These lines identify natural support and resistance price levels in a downward trending market. Figure 7.1 with the June T-Bonds shows the Gann fan drawn from a major high.

The opposite is true in a market trading higher. The beginning of the Gann fan is placed on the low at the beginning of the uptrend. This is illustrated in the June T-Bonds in Figure 7.2.

CROSSING THE LINE

When the market breaks through a Gann line it has a strong tendency to move to the next line. In other words, if the market is trending lower and the price penetrates a Gann support line, it generally continues lower in the direction of the next Gann support line. The June T-Bond chart (Figure 7.3) offers a great illustration of this phenomenon.

The T-Bonds peak at B and quickly break through the Gann line (2×1).

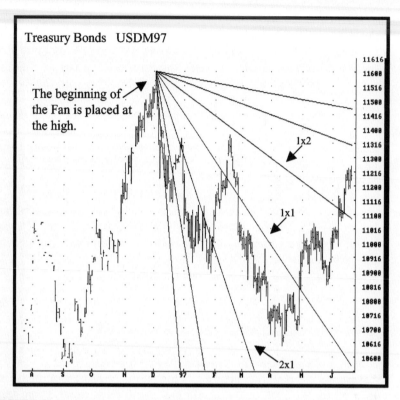

FIGURE 7.1   Gann Fan on Major High

After breaking through this support line, the T-Bonds fall quickly toward the next Gann line (1×1). Although the T-Bonds do not test this lower Gann line (1×1) on the first attempt, the T-Bonds break through the line after a small correction peaks at D. The drop that follows ends at the next Gann line (1×2). Amazingly, the market reverses into a sharp rally from this line (this was also a predetermined Reversal date).

After the T-Bonds reverse at E, notice where the market peaks at F. This peak price is right at a Gann line. From this point (F), the T-Bonds continue the price decline and penetrate three more Gann lines on the way down to the low at G.

Remember, even though there is a strong tendency for markets to be attracted to these Gann lines, it is not a hard-and-fast rule. It will not happen all the time. However, it will happen enough times that it should not be ignored. When the Gann lines are combined with Reversal dates and buy/sell windows, the potential is amazing.

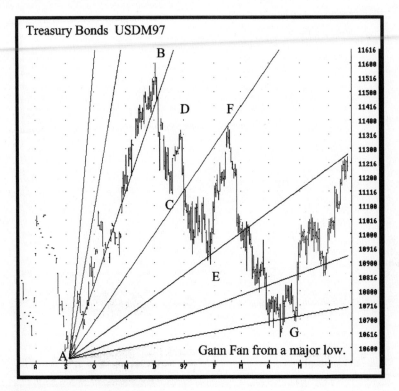

Treasury Bonds USDM97

Gann Fan from a major low.

FIGURE 7.2 Gann Fan on Major Low

1. The major low is marked A.
2. As the trend is up, the beginning of the Gann fan is placed on the low (A).
3. The Gann lines act as support and resistance.

TRADING AGAINST THE GANN LINES

Look at Figure 7.4 of the June T-Bonds. The beginning of the Gann fan is placed at the major low established on September 5 at 105-20 (A). The T-Bonds remain in a very strong upward trend until breaking the Gann line 2×1 at A. This is a signal that the trend is starting to weaken. This also gives notice that the T-Bonds could trade down to the next Gann line, 1×1 (this is the center line). The T-Bonds break through line 1×1 at B. This suggests that the market could attempt to test the lower Gann line, 1×2.

The market finds support at Gann line 1×2 and quickly reverses at E. (This is, after all, a projected Reversal date.) The market rallies sharply

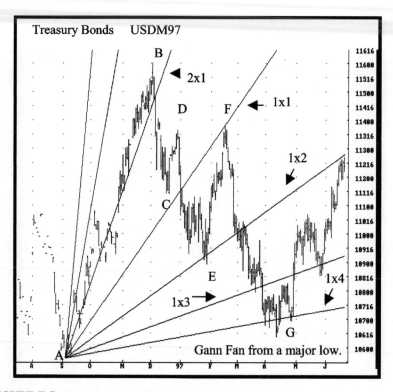

FIGURE 7.3 Gann Fan—Breaking through Support Lines

1. After trading through line 1×1 at C the market trades to the next line, 1×2, at E.

2. The T-Bonds find support at E and resistance at the 1×1 line (F).

3. From the high at F, the T-Bonds trade through the 1×2 line and the 1×3 line and finally find support at the last line, 1×4 (G).

and peaks at the resistance provided by line 1×1 at F. Coincidentally, F is a Reversal date.

Take a look back at Figure 7.3 and locate where the T-Bonds test the Gann line 1×2 at 109-03 on January 27 (E). The T-Bonds are inside the 60 percent buy window. The buy window is based on the move from the low of 105-20 on September 5 (A) to the high of 116-00 on December 3 (B). This means that the market reverses inside the buy window at the Gann support line and on the predicted Reversal date.

Now take a look at the high of 113-25 (F) that occurs on February 28. As you know, this is a predicted Reversal date. In addition, the price is inside the sell window, based on the market move from 116-00 (B) down to 108-30 (E). *Once again, the market reverses inside the sell window, on*

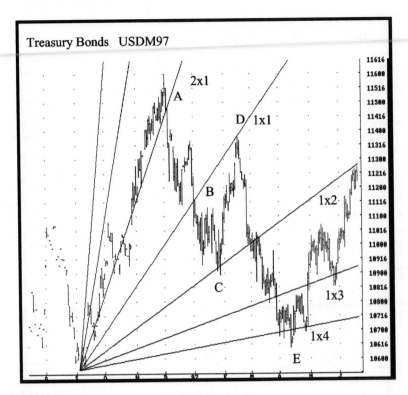

FIGURE 7.4 Gann Line as Support and Resistance

1. After breaking through the 2×1 line at A, the T-Bonds begin a new downward trend to the 1×1 line. The T-Bonds trade through the 1×1 line at B and find support at the 1×2 line.

2. The market reverses at the support provided by line 1×2. (This is also a Reversal date.) This reversal rally peaks at D at the resistance provided by line 1×1. (Again, this is a Reversal date.)

3. At D, the market reverses and continues the downtrend. Each time the T-Bonds break through a lower Gann line, they continue to the next line.

the predicted Reversal date, and at the Gann line. Are you starting to see how this all comes together?

From the high of 113-25 (F), the T-Bonds reverse and resume the downward trend. The market penetrates the Gann line 1×2 again on March 3 at 109-24 and this time falls right through. The T-Bonds continue to trade lower into the next two Gann lines (1×3 and 1×4).

The only time that the T-Bonds do not break through a Gann line and continue lower occurs at Gann line 1×4. Even though the T-Bonds penetrate this line, a buy signal is triggered when the market breaks above the line at G. (G is also a Reversal date.)

TRADING WITH THE GANN LINES

In this section, you will see how Gann lines can be helpful when the market is correcting *against the current trend*. The preceding chapter discussed the markets' tendency to retrace a certain percentage of the original move. In Figure 6.5 of the June T-Bonds, the first correction did not retrace all the way to the 60 percent sell window, but stopped at the 50 percent level. Figure 7.5 shows how you could have known that the 50 percent retracement was actually at resistance and ready to turn.

Gann lines act as magnets that attract the markets to them. In Figure 7.5, the Gann fan begins at the major high at 116-00 (B). After the first initial down move to C, the market begins to trade higher. The market trades up to the Gann line and just penetrates it at D. The next trading day, the T-

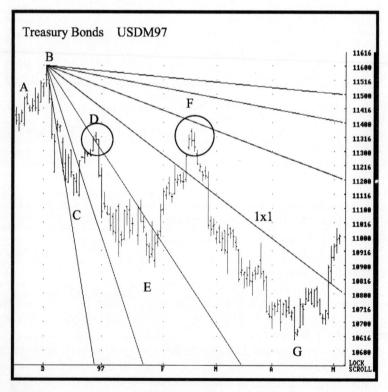

FIGURE 7.5 Gann Lines as Support and Resistance against Current Trend

Bonds open higher and close lower to finish the day as a narrow range day. (*A narrow range day at the end of a market correction is usually a signal that the correction is coming to an end.*) The following day, the T-Bonds fail to continue the upward trend and drop back through the Gann line. This failure is normally a strong sell signal that is followed by a significant price move.

The next time that the T-Bonds test the Gann line is at F when the T-Bonds reach 113-16. (Remember this day was a projected Reversal date and one that was inside the sell window.) In this correction, the market does not touch the Gann line, but it is close enough for the Reversal date to take hold.

When a market is approaching a Gann line, it is very important to watch for this narrow range day. If the price is near a Gann line (it can be just above or below) and a Reversal date is due, be on alert for time and price to come together and trigger a reversal pattern. The strongest signals are generated when the market penetrates a Gann line for one to two days and then drops back through the Gann line. Be especially alert for this when a reversal is due.

Therefore, in Figure 7.5, you know that the 50 percent retracement is the reversal level because as it approaches the Gann line, it trades in a narrow range day on a Reversal day.

I'm going to show you another example using another market. As I was writing this chapter, the Eurocurrency was trading in a strong downward trend. During this bearish trend, the Eurocurrency touched or broke the overhead Gann line three times. However, each time the market penetrated the Gann line, the market reversed to continue the downtrend.

The June Eurocurrency in Figure 7.6 illustrates this perfectly. The market peaks just into the New Year and then begins a new downward trend. After finding support on a lower Gann line, the Eurocurrency rallies up to .9459 (A), penetrating the overhead Gann line. The market fails to follow through with this rally and drops back through the line. Normally, I would expect the market to continue on up to the next Gann line after it breaks the first one. However, I know that when a market does not do what is expected, look for the opposite to happen. That is the case here as the market reverses and collapses.

Once again, after finding support at a lower Gann line, the Eurocurrency rallies through the overhead Gann line to peak at B. This time, the market stays above the line for a few days before dropping through it to continue the downward trend.

The third sell signal occurs at C when the market trades above the Gann line on an intraday time period, but closes below the line to continue the downward trend.

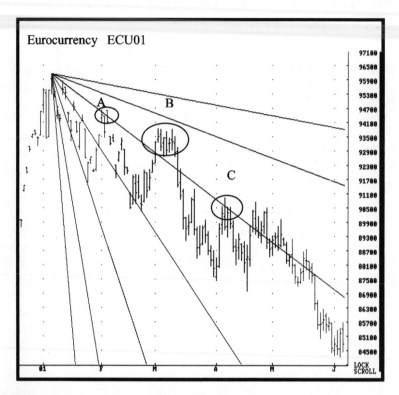

FIGURE 7.6 Gann Lines as Support and Resistance—Eurocurrency
1. The Eurocurrency tests the Gann line at A and then quickly turns lower.
2. The market trades through the Gann line at B. After consolidating for a few days, the Eurocurrency drops through the line and promptly falls to new lows.
3. A small retracement rally reverses at the Gann line at C.

USING THE GANN FAN AND BUY/SELL WINDOWS

In these last couple of chapters, I have talked about buy/sell windows and the Gann fan. Both tools can be used to determine the price levels at which market reversals will most likely occur. You are probably thinking, "Which one is best, and which one should I use?" The answer is that both work very well on their own, but they can also be used together.

After the price level for the buy/sell window has been established, the trader overlays the Gann fan. What usually happens is the market will trade into the buy/sell window and reverse at or near the Gann line. This extra step with the Gann fan allows a trader to be more precise when determining an entry price.

Treasury Bonds

Let's first look at Figures 7.7 and 7.8 in the T-Bonds. (You will notice that these T-Bonds were used earlier to determine Reversal dates.)

In Figure 7.7, the Gann fan is drawn from the major low at A. While making a price correction of the large price move from A to B, the T-Bonds pause briefly at the 1×2 Gann line before continuing down to the 1×3 Gann line. The 1×3 Gann line is sitting just inside the buy window. This combination of Gann support and a predicted Reversal date inside the buy window

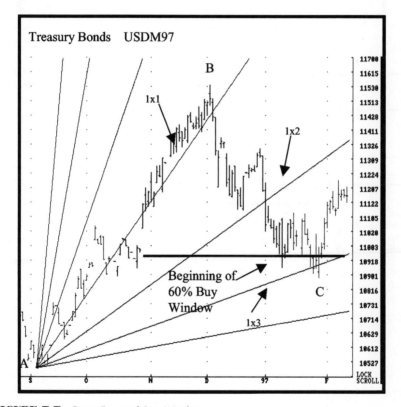

FIGURE 7.7 Gann Fan and Buy Window

1. The Gann fan is drawn from the major low at A.

2. The T-Bonds top at B and trade lower into the 60% buy window.

3. The T-Bonds find support on the 1×3 Gann line. The low at C is a predicted Reversal date. (See Figure 4.4.)

4. The combination of Gann support and a Reversal date inside the 60% buy window proves to be a bullish combination.

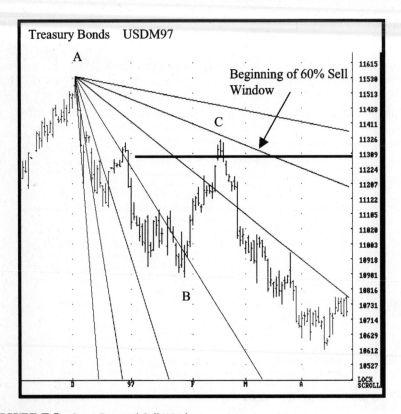

FIGURE 7.8 Gann Fan and Sell Window

1. The Gann fan is drawn from the major high at A.

2. After making a low at B the T-Bonds rally into the 60% sell window.

3. The T-Bonds reverse near the Gann line at C and on a predicted Reversal date. (See Figure 4.5.)

4. This reversal occurs inside the sell window, against the Gann resistance, and on a projected Reversal date.

proves to be a bullish combination. (See Figures 4.4 and 4.5 for projected Reversal dates.)

Cattle

Now we'll look at the April Cattle chart used earlier. Only this time, we will add Gann lines (see Figure 7.9). As Cattle are in an upward trend, we place the beginning of the Gann fan at the low marked B on the chart.

On July 29 at D, the Cattle trade down to a low of 68.15 to establish the

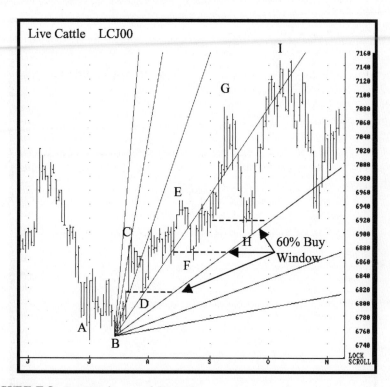

FIGURE 7.9   Buy Windows and Gann Lines

1. The Reaction swing (C to D) touches the 1×1 line at D but just misses the buy window before turning higher.

2. The Reaction swing at E to F reverses inside the buy window.

3. The Reaction swing of G to H reverses right on the Gann line and inside the buy window.

end of the first Reaction swing. The low price of 68.15 did not enter the buy window, but it did touch the Gann line. (Remember the T-Bonds in Figure 7.1. The first Reaction swing did not enter the sell window, but it also turned at the Gann line.) After turning at the Gann line, the Cattle continue the upward trend.

The next time the Cattle test the Gann line occurs at the low of the Reaction swing of G to H. The market hits a low of 69.00 on the projected Reversal date at H. This time, the price is right on the Gann line and inside the buy window. This combination proves to be an extremely good buy signal as the April Cattle rally 2.40 points over the next 13 days. (Remember, Figures 4.2 and 4.3 identified these lows as Reversal dates.)

This is a side note worth mentioning. See where the Cattle peak on the projected Reversal date (I). The rally from the low at H pushes right up to the Gann line, and actually breaks through on the Reversal date. This Reversal date proves to be the high, as a major price decline follows. This is another example of time and price working together for amazing results.

Cotton

Next let's take a look at Figure 7.10 in March Cotton. This is a good example of a strongly trending market in which you'll use the 30 percent retracement. As you can see, the entire downward price move is below the center Gann line.

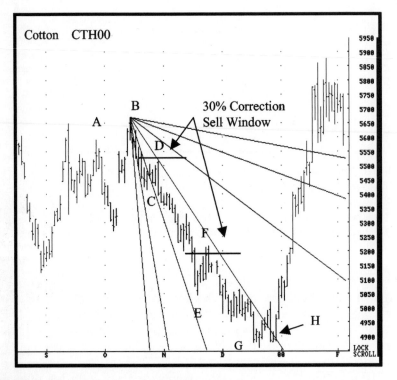

FIGURE 7.10   Sell Window and Gann Fan

1. The first Reaction swing ends and reverses at D. The price at D hits the Gann line and misses the sell window by only a few points.

2. The next Reaction swing pushes into the sell window at F and then drops to new lows.

3. Notice how the strong bearish trend is held intact by the 1×1 line. It is only after breaking the 1×1 line at H that the Cotton can sustain any type of rally.

As Cotton is trending down, the beginning of the Gann fan is placed at the high (B). Cotton begins its first Reaction swing when it trades off of the low at 54.80 (C). This Reaction swing ends at 55.15 (D); it is a retracement of only about 20 percent of the previous market move. This is a characteristic of a strongly trending market where most market corrections are small and short-lived in duration. In this type of scenario, the market usually does not trade inside the sell window. In this example, even though the Cotton does not trade inside the sell window, it reverses precisely on the Gann line to confirm the end of the first Reaction swing.

The Reaction swing at E and F is also a small retracement. From the high at D to the low of 50.45 (E), the Cotton retraces and enters into the sell window. Although that in itself is a good indicator of the reversal price, the Cotton is also bumping up against the center 1×1 Gann line. This helps to reinforce the time and price reversal signal.

Once again, do you notice where this market makes its bottom? It makes the bottom exactly where the center Gann line meets the Reversal date (H). This is another example of time and price working together.

CHAPTER 8

Market Tells

A n old-time trader who was an avid poker player once told me that trading and poker are similar in many ways—but not in the way many people think. New poker players always learn the different hands (card combinations) and the odds of winning with each. They concentrate on betting strategies and the rules of the game. He insisted that even though all this knowledge is necessary and important, it is not the key to becoming a consistent winner. When I asked this old-timer what he meant by this statement, he said, "People; you have to learn to study people. Once you learn this, you can tell what they are about to do without them even knowing they have already given it away." He went on to explain that veteran poker players study the other players at the table. Veteran players play very cautiously at the beginning of a game, and do not start to play aggressively until they have begun to notice small, normally unnoticeable characteristics about their opponents. These can be such things as a player seeming more nervous when he's bluffing, or another who holds his cards differently when he thinks he has a winning hand. Whatever these characteristics are, they can give an edge to the player who is aware enough to identify these tendencies. In the poker world, these tendencies are known as "tells."

The markets are similar to poker players in that the markets also exhibit "tells" or certain characteristics that can give clues to future market price action. If you are aware of the tells, they can forewarn you of a move about to happen. This chapter outlines some "market tells" that are extremely useful when combined with Reversal dates and Action/Reaction.

PATTERNS

Many years ago, I decided to be a technical trader. I wanted to use only the price charts to determine buy and sell signals. I made this decision when I became painfully aware that I was not smart enough to know all the fundamental information of all the markets I wanted to trade. The real problem for me was not getting the news, but knowing how to correctly interpret all of it. I believe this is a problem for many traders. It is difficult to know if you have all the relevant news on a market and how the other major players in the market are interpreting the news. Therefore, I decided that I wanted the market to tell me what it was about to do. It is assumed that the market factors in all the fundamental news and the traders' interpretations of that news. Therefore, current price action should reflect this information. We know that current price action is revealed in chart patterns. I realized that if I could learn to interpret chart patterns with some degree of accuracy, I would have a slight advantage in the market. To succeed, all you really need is a slight advantage—just ask the boys in Las Vegas!

REVERSAL PRICE PATTERNS

In my previous book, *The Traders Handbook: The Reversal Date Phenomenon,* I presented several charting patterns that can be used in conjunction with the Reversal dates to help confirm trading signals. Many traders have since asked me, "Is there an easier way to confirm reversals using fewer patterns?" The answer is yes, I do have an easier way that is very simple and very effective.

For example, let's say that the market is trading lower into the projected Reversal date and I'm looking for a buy signal. The first thing that the market must do on the Reversal date is to trade below the previous day's low. This can be by as little as one point; but it must trade lower than the previous day's low. If the market does not trade below the previous day's low, this usually signals a continuation pattern. (Don't worry, I will talk about this later.) Let's get back to the reversal signals.

On the Reversal date, if the market has traded below the previous day's low, place a buy stop above the daily high of the Reversal day. Leave this order in place for three days. If the buy stop is not filled within three days, cancel the order. Using this approach, you enter the market only when the reversal occurs. If the reversal does not occur, the entry signal is not triggered. (In a market trading higher, the rules are reversed.)

NEW HIGHS ON THE REVERSAL DAY

Let's take a look at Figure 8.1 in the Dow Jones. On Friday, May 18, the Dow closes on the high of the day, 11,418. The following Monday is a projected Reversal date. This means that the Dow would have to trade above Friday's high price of 11,418 before it could be considered as a possible reversal. On the Reversal date the Dow trades to a high of 11,448 before it closes at 11,425. This high of 11,448 is above the previous day's high of 11,418. Therefore, on the "trail day" (the trading day following the reversal

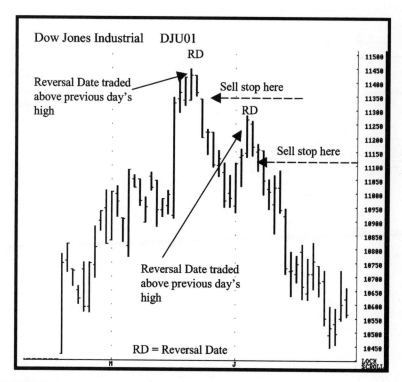

FIGURE 8.1 New High on the Reversal Day

1. On Friday, May 18, the Dow closes on the high of the day. The following Monday is a projected Reversal date. On Monday, the projected Reversal day, the Dow trades above the previous high. (This proves to be the high in the Dow.)

2. As the Dow trades higher on the Reversal date than the previous day's high, place a sell stop under the low of the Reversal day. On the second day following the Reversal day, the Dow trades through the stop price to trigger the sell stop and confirm the sell signal.

date) place a sell stop below the low of the Reversal date. As the low was 11,335, place the sell stop at 11,332 and leave it in the market for three days. On the second day following the Reversal date, the Dow trades through the stop price to confirm the sell signal.

A few days later, the Dow stages a small three-day rally into another Reversal date. On the day prior to the projected Reversal date, the Dow makes a daily high of 11,160. On the Reversal day, the Dow trades to a high of 11,280 and closes at 11,267. This high is above the high of the previous day to set up the reversal pattern. Therefore, on the trail day, enter a sell stop below the low of the Reversal date. Since the low was 11,130, place the sell stop at 11,125. Two days after the Reversal date, the Dow trades through the sell stop to trigger the sell stop and confirm the sell signal and the Reversal date pattern.

FIGURE 8.2 New Low on the Reversal Day

1. On the Reversal day, Wheat trades to a new low (below the previous day's low).

2. The buy stop should be placed above the high of the Reversal day's trading range. In this case, as the high was 248, the stop can be placed at 250.

3. On the following day (the trail day) Wheat gaps higher and trades through the buy stop to confirm the buy signal and the reversal.

NEW LOWS ON THE REVERSAL DAY

Let's look at an example of a new low on the Reversal date (see Figure 8.2). On the projected Reversal date, the Wheat trades to a new contract low; this is below the previous day's low. On the following day, the trail day, enter a buy stop above the high of the Reversal date. Since the high was 248, the buy stop should be placed at 250. (Note: When trading grains, I like to place the stop order more than 2 to 3 cents above the high or below the low.)

The following day, Wheat gaps higher and trades above the previous day's high. Consequently, the buy stop is hit to confirm the Reversal day signal. From this point Wheat trades higher and never looks back.

Even though other patterns can help you enter the market earlier (possibly even at a better price), I feel this trading approach offers a higher degree of reliability. The approach one takes depends on a trader's preference and level of risk tolerance.

OTHER REVERSAL PATTERNS

There are many trading patterns that can be used to help identify tops and bottoms. However, my trading philosophy is to keep it simple. A trader needs to narrow the field and find those price patterns that are simple to use and offer the highest probability of success. Once you have found the patterns, learn them and then use them. You may not catch every top and bottom, but you will catch more than enough.

PEG-LEG

How many times have you heard market experts say, "Buy new contract highs and sell new contract lows"? Even though this saying may be true, tremendous trading opportunities can occur when a market fails to follow through on a new high or low. The *peg-leg* pattern is designed to take advantage of these opportunities.

For this example, we'll say that the market is trading higher and I am waiting for the market to peak and give me a sell signal. What I'm looking for is a market that has just made a new 20-day high. In other words, the market must trade above the highest price of the last 20 trading days. In addition, this new high must be made at least three days after the previous high. Once the market has made this new high, it is time to enter a sell stop that is three to five ticks below the low of this new high day.

Once the market has triggered the sell signal, enter the protective stop three to five ticks above the high of the new high day. As the market begins to move in your favor, money management is up to the individual trader. I have found that every trader has his or her own risk tolerance.

The following is a quick review of the rules for a peg-leg sell signal:

1. The market must make a new 20-day high (it must trade above the highest high of the previous 20 trading days). In addition, this new high must be made at least three days after the previous high. It is best if the market closes above the prior high.

2. When this new high is made, place a sell stop three to five ticks below the low of this new high day. Keep the order working for two days.

3. If filled, place a protective stop three to five ticks above the high of this new high day. (The rules are reversed for a buy signal.)

The following three examples offer very good illustrations of this pattern.

April Hogs

As shown in Figure 8.3, in early May, the April Hogs are in their eighth week of a strong bullish trend. On May 3, the Hogs trade at a high of 60.40 before experiencing a three-day retracement. The Hogs then rally to a new high of 61.05 and close on this day at 60.90. This high satisfies the peg-leg rules—this new high is higher than the high of the previous 20 trading days, and the new high is made four days after the previous high.

Conventional thinking says, "Wow, a new high—this market is ready to take off." However, as you can see, no follow-through buying occurs the next day.

It is very important to remember that when a market does not behave the way you are expecting, it is time to exit because the market is about to do the opposite. In this example the Hogs reverse to trigger the sell signal when the price hits the sell stop resting below the low of the new high day. As you can see, this marks the beginning of a major price collapse in the Hog market—a great trade for anyone on the short side.

Dow Jones

This next example (Figure 8.4) is quite amazing. I say this because the peg-leg pattern triggered a sell signal at the very top of the greatest bull market in Dow history.

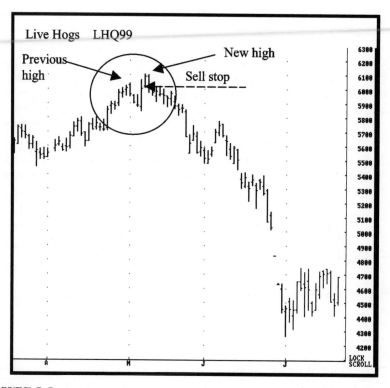

FIGURE 8.3 Peg-Leg

1. In early May, the Hogs make a new high at 60.40 that is followed by a three-day correction.

2. The Hogs rally to another high that is above the previous high at 60.40. This is the new high day.

3. When new buying fails to materialize the market reverses to trigger the sell signal. This is the beginning of a price collapse in the Hogs.

On January 14, 2000, the March Dow Jones futures traded to a new contract high of 11,840 (2) before closing that day at 11,835. This new high was made four days after the previous high of 11,770 (1). The following day, as the commentators on CNN were touting the Dow at 12,000, I watched the Dow open lower and trade below the new high day's low. This confirmed a major sell signal and also marked the end of the bull run.

We will look at one more example before moving on to the next pattern.

FIGURE 8.4   Peg-Leg in the Dow

1. On January 14, the March Dow makes a new high (2) at 11,840. This is higher than the previous high of 11,770 (1) made just a few days earlier.

2. A sell stop is placed underneath the low of the new high day.

3. The following day, the Dow trades through the sell stop to confirm the sell signal and a major top in the market.

Pork Bellies

As shown in Figure 8.5, a strong bull market ends when the July Bellies trade to a new high on April 2 (2) and closes higher than the previous high on March 27 (1). Two days later, the Bellies trade below the low of the new high day to trigger the sell signal and the end of the bull market.

(Note: Look at the trading day just before the new high day. It also traded to a new high but did not *close* above the previous high (1). Therefore, day 2, with the closing price above the previous high, is the correct day to use.)

Five days after the peg-leg formation confirms the sell signal, the Bel-

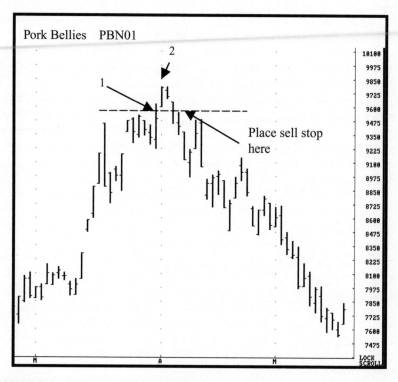

FIGURE 8.5 Peg-Leg in the Pork Bellies

1. On March 27, the Bellies make a high of 95.25 (1). This high is followed by a two-day correction.

2. On April 2, the Bellies rally to a new high of 97.87 (2) and close above the previous high (1).

3. Two days later, the Bellies trade below the low of the new high day (2). This confirms the sell signal and marks the end of the bull market.

lies complete a Reaction swing and the beginning of a new Reaction cycle. This is all illustrated in Figure 8.5.

GAP AND GO

In 1993, a successful doctor opened an account with me at Traders Network. He funded his account with $12,000 and began to place orders periodically. A few weeks later, he called and said, "I have been testing you and your firm. I like what you have done for me so far and I want to deposit more money into my account so that I can increase my trading." He immediately brought his account balance up to approximately $70,000.

After not trading for a few days, he called one morning right after the metals had opened and asked me to buy 20 contracts of Silver. For the next few days, he continued to add to his position.

The good doctor (that's what we called him) had just bought Silver at the exact bottom of a major rally. Soon after, he added positions in Gold, Sugar, and Coffee that all had the same results. In roughly two months his account balance peaked at around $1,500,000—not bad for eight weeks of work! And as Paul Harvey often says, "Now for the rest of the story," because there is more to this story.

The good doctor had a large portion of the profits wired to his bank account. In addition, he was stopped out of most of his positions on a very volatile trading day following a three-day weekend. These two events dropped his account balance to just under $100,000.

For a few days, the good doctor lay low and waited for the next trading opportunity to present itself. He didn't wait long. Soon he began to buy Soybeans just as aggressively as he had bought the Silver. Once again, he had entered a market at a major low and just before a substantial rally. He continued to add positions as the Soybeans moved higher and exited just after the Soybeans topped (about six weeks after his entry). The good doctor's story is an incredible one. Twice in a six-month time span he grew his account from under $100,000 to over $1,500,000!

Not everyone has a $100,000 account to trade with, or can trade as aggressively as the good doctor. However, what you can do is use the same price pattern that he used to identify his entry points in these markets. I call this pattern the *gap and go*.

An old adage says to buy new highs and sell new lows. The gap and go pattern is a direct variation of this adage, as the gap and go kicks in when these new levels fail. When the market fails to follow through on a breakout, the reversals can be significant. Once you have learned the rules for this pattern, you will begin to see it pop up in several markets.

The rules for a gap and go buy signal are:

1. On day 1, the market needs to trade lower than the previous day's low and close lower than the opening price. (The more closely the market closes to the low of the daily trading range, the better.)

2. On day 2, the market needs to open higher than the closing price of day 1. In addition, the entire trading range of day 2 should be above the closing price of day 1.

3. The closing price of day 2 needs to be above the high of day 1. If this condition is met, place a buy stop above the high of day 2.

4. A buy signal is triggered when the market trades above the high of day 2 and hits the buy stop.

The rules are reversed for sell signals.

The gap and go pattern will often occur at major tops and bottoms; and it is usually followed by a sharp market move. Once the rules are learned, it is easily recognized. Every trader should be aware and on the lookout for the gap and go—don't leave home without it!

December T-Bonds

As shown in Figure 8.6, on September 24 (1), the T-Bonds open higher than the previous day's high and close near the top of the daily range, giving all

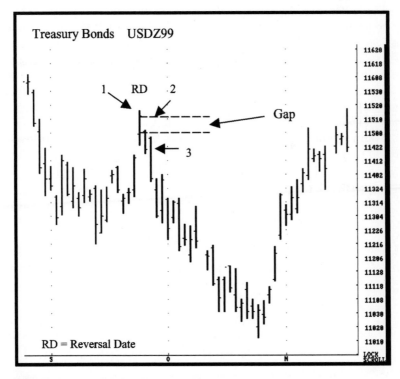

FIGURE 8.6 Gap and Go

1. On day 1, the T-Bonds gap up, opening higher and closing above the previous day's high.

2. The following day (2), the T-Bonds open lower and close below the previous day's low. On day 3, the sell stop under the low of day 2 is triggered.

the appearances of a market ready to continue to new highs. The following day (2), T-Bonds open lower and close below the low of the previous trading day (1). The entire trading range of day 2 is below the previous day's closing price. On trading day 3, T-Bonds trade lower, triggering the sell signal and marking the beginning of a $4,000 price decline.

July Wheat

On December 13 (1), July Wheat (Figure 8.7) drops to a new contract low and closes lower than the opening price. The following day (2) the Wheat gaps higher and closes above the previous day's high. The entire trading range of day 2 is above the previous day's closing price, leaving the opening gap unfilled. The next day Wheat trades higher, hits the buy stop, and confirms the buy signal. This is the beginning of a price rally in the Wheat.

FIGURE 8.7 Gap and Go—Wheat

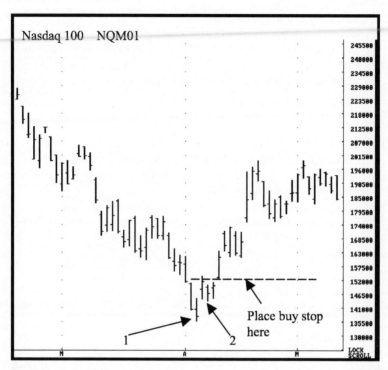

FIGURE 8.8 Gap and Go—Nasdaq

Nasdaq

On April 4 (1), the June Nasdaq (Figure 8.8) drops to a new contract low (lower than the previous low) and closes lower than the opening price. The next trading day (2), it opens higher than the previous day's close and closes higher than the previous day's high. The daily trading range of day 2 was also above the close of day 1. This leaves the gap unfilled. The buy stop is not triggered until two days after it was placed when the Nasdaq finally trades higher.

GAP REVERSAL

This pattern is well known and has been described in numerous trading books and courses. However, it works so well with the Reversal dates that I include it in all my seminars and educational material. The pattern is called the gap reversal.

The rules for a buy signal are:

1. On day 1, the market needs to make a new low that is below the low of the previous day.
2. On day 2, the market needs to open lower than the previous day's low and close higher than its opening price.
3. The opening price of day 2 should be at or very close to the low of the day.
4. If the first three rules are met, place a buy stop above the high of day 1.

Rules are reversed for sell signals.

Let's now go through some examples of the gap reversal.

On day 1, the April Cattle (Figure 8.9) trade to a new low and close near the low of the day. The following day (2), the Cattle open lower than the previous day's low and quickly rally. A buy signal is confirmed when

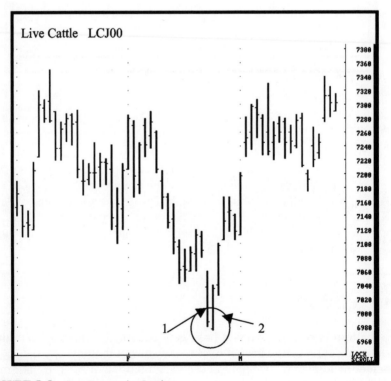

FIGURE 8.9 Gap Reversal—Cattle

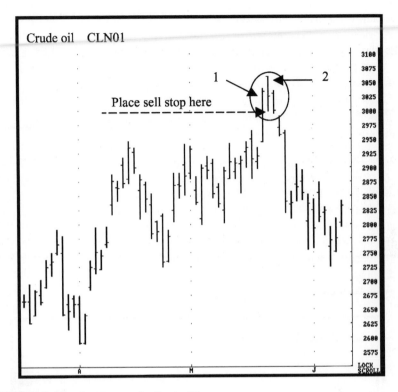

Crude oil   CLN01

Place sell stop here

FIGURE 8.10   Gap Reversal—Crude Oil

the April Cattle trade above the high of day 2. As you can see, the Cattle rally over 2.50 points during the next seven days.

On day 1 in Figure 8.10, the Crude Oil hits a high of 30.39. On day 2, the market opens at a new high that is higher than the previous day's high. This is followed by a reversal and a closing price lower than the opening price. On day 3, the Crude Oil trades below the low of day 2, to trigger the sell signal and confirm a major high.

TRAIL DAY

The dates of projected Reversal dates are specific and precise. The preceding sections have just given you specific and objective patterns that must be met in order for a Reversal date to be confirmed. If the specific criteria are not met on the predicted Reversal date, then look at the next trading day. I call this the "trail day." The trail day is a directional indicator. The direction in which the market closes on the trail day is usually the direction of the next price move. In other words, on the trail day, if the market closes higher than the opening price, the market will usually begin to trade higher over the next few days. If the market closes lower than the opening price, the market will tend to trade lower.

This rule holds true for a high percentage of the time and should not be ignored. I also use the trail day as an additional confirmation of the Reversal date. If a Reversal date signal confirms a buy signal and the trail day closes higher than the opening price, chances are increased that the reversal will continue with good follow-through buying. However, if the Reversal date has confirmed a buy signal but the trail day closes lower than the opening price, I will make sure my protective stop is in place and I may even tighten it to reduce the risk. This type of monitoring should be an important aspect of your money management.

Let's examine some examples to see how the trail day confirms market direction, using the same three markets used earlier—Cattle, T-Bonds, and Cotton.

The trail day is marked TD in Figure 8.11. (By looking at each trail day

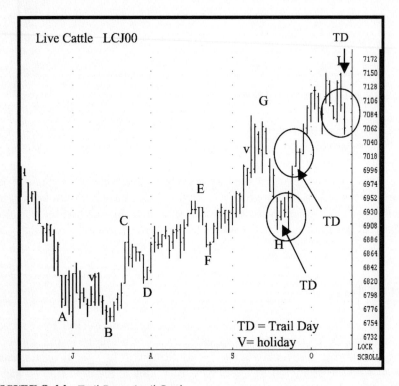

FIGURE 8.11 Trail Day—April Cattle

in the Cattle, you can determine future market direction with a fairly high degree of accuracy.) From the major low at B to the major high at I, each Reversal date is confirmed, with the one exception at G. At G, the Reversal date is not confirmed by any initial pattern. When this happens, you look at the trail day. The trail day closes higher than the opening price, suggesting higher prices, but fails to follow through.

Starting with the major high identified by B, the T-Bonds in Figure 8.12 close lower than the opening price on the trail day, indicating lower prices. At C the market closes higher than the opening price on the trail day. This turns the market higher. At D, the rally from C is reversed as the trail day closes lower than the open.

After hitting a low on the Reversal date at E, the trail day closes higher than the opening price and gives the green light to a strong rally that ends when the trail day at F closes lower than the opening price. This leads to a sustained price decline in the T-Bonds.

After each Reversal date in Cotton in Figure 8.13, the direction of the trail day close confirms the future direction of the market.

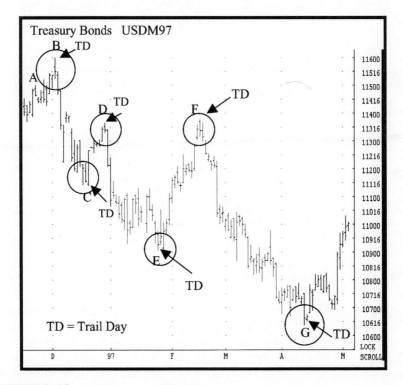

FIGURE 8.12   Trail Day—June T-Bonds

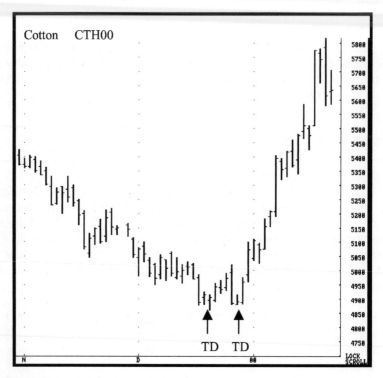

FIGURE 8.13   Trail Day—March Cotton

By now you can see the value of the trail date as a directional indicator. It can also be a useful tool when incorporating money management. After a sell reversal is confirmed, place a protective stop three to five ticks above whichever is higher—the Reversal date high or the trail day high. After a buy reversal, place a protective stop three to five ticks below whichever is lower—the Reversal day low or the trail day low.

CONTINUATION PATTERNS

Not every predicted Reversal date is going to result in a major change in trend or a significant top or bottom in the market. Sometimes the market will break out of a price consolidation area after trading in a range, or it will break above a resistance level or below a support level. This type of price action will usually be followed by a price move in the same direction as the current trend. Knowing where these breakouts should occur will allow traders to properly position themselves and to gain an advantage in the market. I call these continuation patterns.

There are three price patterns that I use to identify continuation patterns. Knowing when the current trend will continue is just as valuable as knowing when the market will reverse.

GAPPING PATTERN

The gapping pattern is identified by a breakaway gap. A breakaway gap is just what the name implies—a gap on the price chart caused by a breaking away from a support or resistance level. A market will gap up if a large influx of buy orders is waiting to be executed at the opening bell and sell orders are lacking. The opposite is true for a market that gaps lower on the open (a large influx of sell orders on the open with a lack of buy orders).

A breakaway gap almost always occurs after a market has tested a support or resistance level. Typically, the breakaway gap marks the beginning of another big move.

On the projected Reversal date or trail day, if the market gaps in the direction of the prevailing trend and the gap is left unfilled by the end of the trading day, the market will usually continue to trade in that direction for a minimum of two to three days.

Let's say that the market has been trading higher for several days and is now testing resistance from a previous high. In addition, the market has been trading sideways for a few days as it approaches the projected Reversal date. On the Reversal date the market gaps higher, above the resistance price level, and trades higher for the remainder of the day. Therefore, the gap is left unfilled at the end of the trading day. Based on this gapping pattern, I know with a high degree of reliability that the market should continue to trade higher for the next two to three days. Often, these two or three days of trading will lead to a large price move.

The rules are reversed for sell signals.

Let's take a look at some examples of the gapping pattern.

The Crude Oil in Figure 8.14 has just entered into the sell window. The market trades sharply lower on the predicted Reversal day. The Crude Oil gaps lower on the trail day and closes lower than the opening price. The Crude Oil continues to trade lower for the next four days.

The Pork Bellies in Figure 8.15 have been trading higher for several days. Just before the scheduled Reversal day, the market retraces for two days. On the Reversal day, the Bellies open higher, leaving a gap, and then continue to trade higher for the rest of the day. The Bellies never pull back to fill the gap. Instead, they continue higher for the next six days.

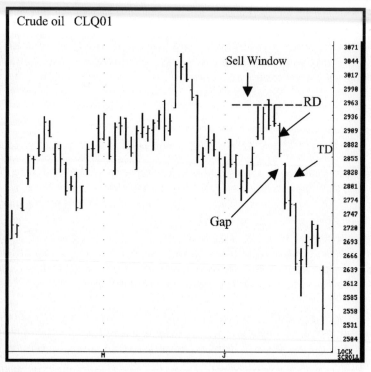

FIGURE 8.14 Gapping Pattern—Crude Oil

STRONG ADVANCE

Just before I sat down to write this section, I read an e-mail advertising a very expensive seminar being offered by a well-known market guru. In this seminar, he was going to teach you a price pattern that he had discovered. He claimed that it would make you extremely wealthy. In the e-mail he said that he had used this pattern recently to identify a buy signal in the S&P 500. By entering the market on this buy signal, you would have been long the S&P just before Alan Greenspan of the Federal Reserve lowered interest rates on April 18. Of course, I looked up the S&P chart and found April 18. Lo and behold, what did I see? A pattern that I wrote about a couple of years earlier in *The Traders Handbook: The Reversal Date Phenomenon* called the strong advance price pattern. Using the rules I am about to outline, a buy signal would have been confirmed one day before Mr. Greenspan lowered interest rates on April 18. Incredibly, this was followed by a one-day rally of over 70.00 points in the June S&P. That is a nice chunk of change!

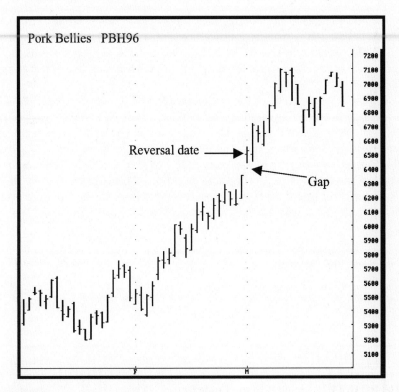

FIGURE 8.15 Gapping Pattern—Pork Bellies

Now that I have piqued your interest, I will get right to the setup rules for the strong advance pattern. These rules are for a buy signal in an uptrending market.

1. In an uptrending market, day 1 should close lower than the opening price (this is against the current trend).
2. On day 2, the market should close higher than the opening price (in same direction of the current trend).
3. On day 3 (this works best if day 3 is also a projected Reversal date) the market should close lower than the opening price (against the current trend, similar to day 1). On day 4, place a buy stop above the high of day 3.

The rules are reversed for a sell pattern.

I look for this pattern whenever the market approaches a support or resistance level. It seems that demand increases at support or resistance, and when the market breaks through, the rush to enter is great. I like this pattern because it is usually followed by a strong price move in the direction of the prevailing trend. As mentioned before, the best results with this pattern occur when the third day of the pattern is a projected Reversal date.

Figure 8.16 is a chart of the infamous June S&P mentioned earlier. The market had been trading higher after making a bottom five days earlier. On day 1, the S&P opened higher and closed lower (against the current upward trend). The high of day 1 is near a resistance level that was established approximately two weeks earlier. On day 2, the market opened lower and closed higher (in the same direction of the current trend). Day 3 saw the market open lower and close even lower than the opening price. The high on day 3 was 1192.50, and the direction of the close versus the

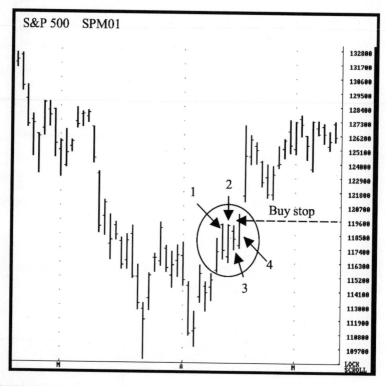

FIGURE 8.16 Strong Advance—June S&P

1. The pattern (days 1, 2, 3) develops near a resistance price level. It is time to place a buy stop on day 4 just above the high of day 3. On day 4 (April 17), the S&P trades above the high of day 3 to trigger the buy signal at 1193.00.

2. On April 18, the Fed lowers interest rates, triggering a strong one-day advance.

opening was against the prevailing trend. The setup for the strong advance pattern was now complete.

On April 18, Mr. Greenspan (without warning) lowered interest rates and the S&P took off like a rocket. The S&P hit a high price of 1270.00 and settled the day at 1246.00.

You may be asking, "Did the Dow Jones give the same buy signal?" Yes, it did! Let's look at Figure 8.17 showing the June Dow Jones. The Dow had also been trending higher as it approached day 1. On day 1, the Dow opened higher and closed lower (against the current trend). On day 2, the Dow opened lower and closed higher (in the direction of the trend). On

FIGURE 8.17 Strong Advance—Dow Jones

1. On day 1, the Dow closes lower than the opening price (against the current trend).

2. On day 2, the Dow closes higher than the opening price (in the direction of the current trend).

3. One day 3, the Dow closes lower than the opening price (against the current trend).

4. On day 4, the Dow trades above the high of day 3 to trigger the buy signal.

day 3, the Dow opened lower and closed even lower than the opening price (against the current trend). Now, just like the S&P, the setup was complete. It was time to enter a buy stop just above the high of day 3.

On day 4, the Dow futures contract traded to a high of 10,210 to fill the buy stop and give the trader a long position at around 11,960. The following day, after Mr. Greenspan's surprise announcement, the Dow surged to a high of 10,700 before it closed the day at 10,650. At $10 per point in the Dow, you can figure the potential gains available from this signal.

Let's get away from the stock indexes and look at a different market. For this example, I will use Cotton in Figure 8.18.

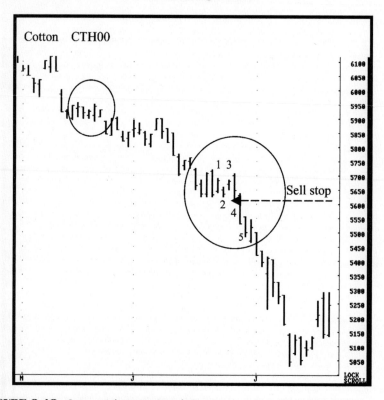

FIGURE 8.18   Strong Advance—March Cotton

1. On day 1, Cotton closes higher than the opening price (against the current downward trend).

2. On day 2, Cotton closes lower than the opening price (in the same direction as the current trend).

3. On day 3, Cotton closes higher than the opening price. On day 4, a sell stop is placed below the low of day 2.

4. It is not until day 5 that the Cotton trades below the low of day 2 to confirm the sell signal and the continuation of the trend.

March Cotton has been trending lower for quite some time before it begins to form a sideways pattern in late June. This pattern actually forms an extended strong advance pattern. On day 1, the Cotton closes higher than the opening price (against the trend). On day 2, the market closes lower than the opening price. (See how the level of support begins to form under the lows of the last few days.) On day 3, the Cotton closes higher than the opening price (against the trend). But it is not until day 5 that the Cotton finally breaks below the support and begins a new push to much lower prices.

Can you find another strong advance pattern in this Cotton chart?

MAJOR REVERSAL

The final pattern to be discussed is called the major reversal. It is a simple but very powerful pattern. It usually appears at major turning points in the market—after the market has just made a new contract low or a new contract high. Just like some of the other patterns discussed, the major reversal goes against the old saying "Buy new highs and sell new lows."

This pattern is most effective when the market is moving into a projected Reversal date; but it does not have to fall exactly on a Reversal date to generate a good signal. The major reversal can also be found at the end of market corrections.

The rules for the major reversal pattern are very simple. The rules for a buy signal are:

1. The market needs to make a new 10-day low.

2. As it heads into the Reversal date, the market needs to close lower than the opening price for at least three days in a row. (The days are numbered in Figure 8.19.)

3. After the close of the third day or before the opening of the fourth day, enter a buy stop just above the daily high of day 3. Leave the stop in place for two days.

4. If the market does not trigger the buy stop and the market closes lower than the opening price for day 4, reenter the buy stop above the high of day 4. Continue this procedure as long as the market continues to close lower than the opening price.

5. Once the long position is confirmed by the buy stop being hit, place the protective sell stops below the contract low. (Figures 8.19 to 8.21 offer good illustrations of this pattern in action.)

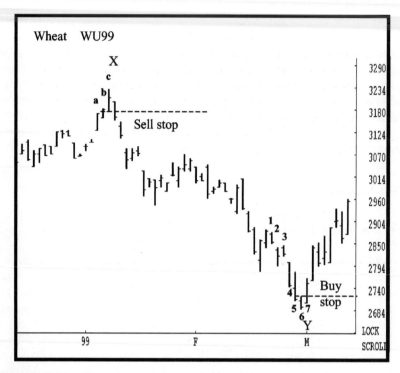

FIGURE 8.19   Major Reversal—September Wheat

1. Sell signal (X)—Days a, b, and c all close higher than the opening price.

2. A sell signal is triggered when the market trades below the low of day c.

3. Buy signal (Y)—The market closes lower than the open for six days in a row. On day 4, a buy stop is placed above the high of day 3. This process is continued until the high is penetrated—this finally occurs on day 7.

September Wheat

In late February, September Wheat (Figure 8.19) has just formed a three-day Reaction swing (ending at 1). From 1, the market trades lower and closes lower than the open for three days straight. Normally, I would look at this as a possible setup pattern for a major reversal; however, in this case the Wheat does not make a new low on day 3. On day 4, Wheat opens lower, continues lower for the rest of the trading session, and closes lower than the opening price. The setup is complete.

A buy stop is placed just above the high of day 4, but the market continues lower. However, on day 5, the Wheat makes another new contract low, and it closes lower than the opening price. Even though the buy signal is not triggered, the market is still set up for a possible major reversal. Therefore, the buy stop would be placed above the high of day 5.

On day 6, the Wheat drops to yet another new contract low, and it closes lower than the opening price. Following the same procedure, the buy stop is placed above the high of day 6.

Finally, patience pays off as the market opens higher on March 1 (day 7), and trades above the high of day 6 for the remainder of the day. This price action triggers the buy stop and confirms the buy signal. (You may also recognize this as a gap and go pattern.) However you look at it, the major reversal provides the signal to buy the Wheat at the major bottom so you can enter at the beginning of the new trend.

June Nasdaq

I think that you will find Figure 8.20 very interesting. It is a chart of the June Nasdaq 100 at the height of the Internet craze (this was also touted as

FIGURE 8.20 Major Reversal—June Nasdaq

1. The three trading days prior to the new contract high (4) all closed higher than the opening price.

2. A sell stop is placed below the low of day 4. The sell stop is elected on the second down day. This is followed by a steep price decline.

the strongest bull market in history). Previous examples have shown charts of the Dow Jones and the S&P 500. Both examples demonstrate market tells that were used to identify market reversals at the point of trend exhaustion. The Nasdaq is yet another example of a market saying sell when the public was saying buy.

On March 15, the Nasdaq 100 has just completed a three-day correction from the high established on March 10. The Nasdaq 100 quickly recovers from the correction as it resumes the bullish trend to push to a new contract high on March 24 (4). This proves to be the all-time high in the June Nasdaq 100.

Now let's go back and see how this market sets up for the major reversal pattern. It starts four days before the major high on March 24. On March 21 (1), the Nasdaq 100 opens lower and closes higher than the opening price. This day is marked day 1 on Figure 8.20.

This is followed by days 2, 3, and 4, which also close higher than the opening price—the setup pattern for the major reversal pattern is complete. Therefore, a sell stop would be placed under the low of day 4.

The next day is an inside day that does not trade below the daily low of day 4. Therefore, the sell signal is not triggered. The sell stop is left in place another day. (I usually like to leave it in place two days.)

Finally, on the following day, the Nasdaq 100 trades below the low of the preceding day to trigger the sell signal and mark the end of one of the strongest bull markets in history.

December Cattle

The December Cattle (Figure 8.21) had two major reversal patterns develop in a six-week period. One marked the end of a sharp price decline; the second pattern identified the end of a strong rally. Let's first talk about the major low.

On May 7, the December Cattle trade to a new contract low and close lower than the opening price (3). Two days later (5), a buy signal is generated by the major reversal pattern. Before going any further, let's see how this buy signal was set up by this reversal pattern.

On May 5, the Cattle broke below support provided by a double bottom formation and closed lower than the opening price and at a new contract low (day 1). The Cattle made new lows each of the following two days (2 and 3). (They both also closed lower than the opening price.) The market is now set up for a possible major reversal. A buy stop is placed above the high of day 3. Once again, the market trades lower and closes lower than the open. Because the buy stop is unfilled, the buy stop is lowered to just above the high of day 4.

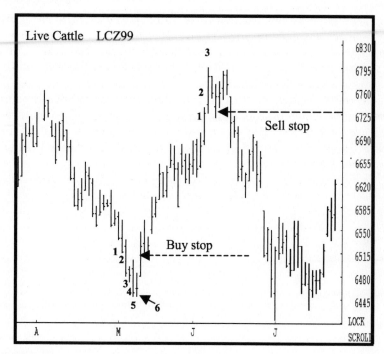

FIGURE 8.21   Major Reversal—December Cattle

On day 5, the Cattle rally early in the trading session to trigger the buy stop and initiate a long position. The rally quickly fails and the market drops to a new low to cause a small loss on the trade. (This is why protective stops are placed as soon as the entry signal is confirmed.)

Looking at the chart reveals that the market is still set up for a major reversal. Even though the last buy signal failed and caused a small loss, the market dropped to a new low and closed lower than the opening price. This means that a new buy stop should be placed above the high of day 6.

Even though we would suffer an initial small loss on this trade, staying with the major reversal pattern would be well worth the wait. When the second buy stop is triggered above the high of day 6, the Cattle rally for 19 days! Coincidentally, the rally ends as a result of a major reversal pattern. Let's take a look at this one and see how it set up.

On June 3, the Cattle trade above 66.97 and break out of a consolidation pattern (1). This results in a new high for the Cattle as the market closes higher than the opening price. The same thing happens for the next two trading days, before the market finally tops at 67.95 on June 7 (3). The setup is now complete. (The market is trading at a new high after trading for three straight days in a row with the closing prices higher than the opens.) A sell stop is now placed just below the low of day 3.

It takes two days for the market to trigger the sell price and confirm the sell signal at 67.25 on June 9 (4). However, the market does not continue lower. It challenges the contract high and peaks at 67.90, just shy of the contract high of 67.95. The protective stops are never hit and the Cattle turn south. This major reversal pattern is followed by a price collapse in the Cattle. Figure 8.21 offers a very good illustration of the major reversal pattern.

CHAPTER 9

Time, Price, and Pattern Working Together

T hroughout this book, I have illustrated how time and price can influence market action. There are many experts who use only time and price to determine market reversals. While this may work well, I am a strong believer in finding the very best way to confirm a trade. When time and price are confirmed by an identifiable price pattern, the signals become more reliable. I will refer to the three markets that we have looked at before to show how incorporating price patterns with time and price helps to confirm buy and sell signals.

Cattle

To see how this works, let's review the April Cattle in Figure 9.1. Remember that the Reversal dates in the second half of the Reaction cycle were projected from the first half of the Reaction cycle.

The three Reversal dates at F, H, and I confirm market reversals. The projected Reversal date of September 24 results in a continuation pattern indicating the trend should continue higher into I.

On August 23 (F), the Cattle trade below the previous day's low and close at 68.75. You can now place a buy stop just above the daily high of the Reversal day.

The following day (the trail day) the Cattle close higher than the opening price, suggesting that the market is ready to turn higher. *Remember, the market will usually trade in the same direction that the trail day closes versus the opening price.*

On August 24 (the trail day, after F), the April Cattle trade above the

131

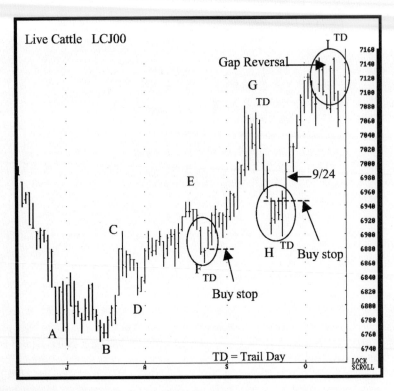

FIGURE 9.1   Time, Price, and Pattern—April Cattle

1. The Cattle make a low at F. This is followed by a buy signal that sends the Cattle to a high at G.

2. The Cattle trade lower into a predicted Reversal date (H). The combination of time, price, and pattern triggers another buy signal that is followed by a move to higher prices into (I).

3. The gap reversal pattern on the projected Reversal day at I results in a strong market reversal and the beginning of a new downtrend.

high and through the buy stop. This confirms the Reversal pattern and the beginning of the rally in the Cattle. This rally ends 13 days later when the Cattle peak at 70.70.

Take a close look at the price pattern at F. Can you see the gap and go pattern? The market opens higher than the closing price of the trail day; the entire trading range is above the previous close; and the closing price is above the high of the trail day. This gap and go pattern is another confirmation of this reversal in Cattle.

The Cattle make a new low on the predicted Reversal date (H). Therefore, you would place a buy stop above the high of the Reversal date (in this case, above 69.50).

On the trail day, Cattle close higher than the opening price. This indicates higher prices should follow. The day after the trail day, the Cattle trade above the high of the Reversal date to trigger the buy signal at 69.60 and the start of another rally in the April Cattle.

Another projected Reversal date falls on September 24. On this date, the Cattle trade above the high of the previous day. This sets up the potential of a downside reversal. However, on the trail day, the market closes higher than it opened. As the price action on the trail day is a good indicator of future price direction, the Cattle should continue higher; this is a continuation pattern.

Fifteen trading days after triggering the buy signal at 69.60 (H), the Cattle complete the rally at 71.32, only one day before the next predicted Reversal date of October 13 (I). On the projected Reversal date (I), April Cattle finish the Reaction cycle with a bearish gap reversal pattern.

Using projected Reversal dates and confirmation patterns, the knowledgeable trader could have bought the low (H) and sold the high (I) of this large price move in the Cattle. Just like the old saying goes, "Buy low, sell high."

Treasury Bonds

The June T-Bonds contract in Figure 9.2 offers some great illustrations of pattern confirmations on projected Reversal dates. We'll focus on the Reversal dates at E, F, and G.

The Reaction swing of C to D projects a Reversal date for January 27. On this date (E), the T-Bonds trade below the low of the previous day's low and close below the open. This sets up a possible reversal. A buy order would be placed above the high of this Reversal date. As I like to place orders at least three ticks above the high, I would place the buy stop at 109-27 (three ticks above the high of 109-24).

On the trail day, the T-Bonds trade high enough to trigger the buy signal at 109-27. Following this reversal, the market rallies strongly. The rally ends on another Reversal date at the high of 113-25 (F).

Two patterns help to verify the reversal signal at (F). These are the gap reversal pattern and the trade below the low of the Reversal date. In addition, as the market closes lower than the opening on the trail day, this reversal enjoys a third confirmation.

These three price patterns help to verify the reversal at F. Once the

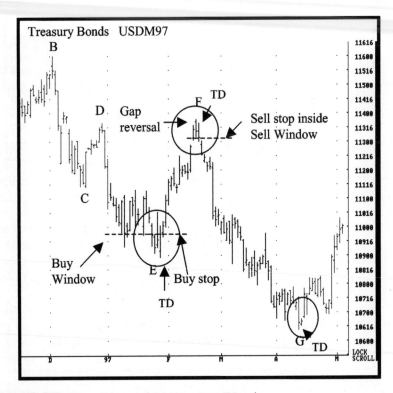

FIGURE 9.2   Time, Price, and Pattern—June T-Bonds

1. The T-Bonds make a new low on the projected Reversal day at E. (This is also inside a buy window.) The buy signal is triggered when the T-Bonds trade above the Reversal day high.

2. A gap reversal pattern, combined with the Reversal day inside the sell window, results in a major price reversal at F.

3. On the trail day, the T-Bonds close higher than the opening price, adding yet another confirmation of a major bottom and the end of the Reaction cycle at G.

short position is entered at 113-00, an extended price decline occurs down to 106-12. The price decline ends on yet another Reversal date—a date that had been forecast weeks in advance.

Cotton

The gap reversal pattern is very evident in the March Cotton (Figure 9.3). The gap reversal occurs at the major top at B when the Cotton opens higher than the previous day's high and closes lower than its

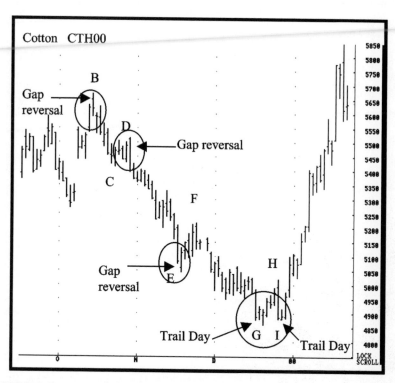

FIGURE 9.3 Time, Price, and Pattern—March Cotton

1. A major high is confirmed with a gap reversal pattern at B. A peg-leg pattern also forms at this new high (B).

2. The gap reversal pattern confirms the Reversal date at D to trigger the continuation of the downward trend. The gap reversal pattern at E is the beginning of a new Reaction swing.

3. The double bottoms at G and I are confirmed by the trail days that both close higher than their opening prices.

opening price. Therefore, the gap reversal pattern confirms the reversal at B.

This same pattern appears again at D. On October 28, Cotton opens higher than the previous day's high, and it closes lower than the previous day's low. This is a strong gap reversal pattern. The following day, Cotton continues to trade lower. This completes the first Reaction swing and confirms a continuation of the downward trend.

CHAPTER 10

When the Patterns Do Not Match Exactly

Just like everything else in life, the market is not perfect and exact. If it were, life would be easy and so would trading. There are times when the forward and reverse counts do not match up exactly; even though this can cause frustration, it doesn't have to. Occasionally, a calculated Reversal date will fall in the middle of a trending market and there will be no Reaction swing. In Figure 10.1 of the Dow Jones futures contract, I will illustrate how to handle this situation.

March Dow Jones

On January 14, 2000, a Reversal date, the March Dow Jones futures in Figure 10.1 rallied to a new high of 11,840 (B) and closed at 11,835. As the closing price was above the high of the previous day, everyone was excited and ready to buy the next day. However, this raised a red flag for me because this day was a projected Reversal date and, therefore, could be the beginning of a market reversal. The next day, the Dow opened lower and traded below the Reversal date low; in fact, this day's entire trading range was below the previous day's closing price—both a gap and go and a peg-leg pattern. Since this was also a predetermined Reversal date, these confirmation signals were very significant—B proved to be a major top.

After confirming this reversal to trigger a sell signal at 11,700, the Dow continued its sharp price decline to a low of 10,779 on January 28 (C). A two-day rally followed that ended on February 1 (D) to complete the first Reaction swing of C to D.

Now that the first Reaction swing has been identified, it is time to do a

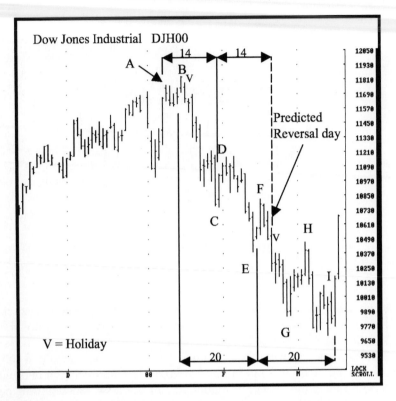

FIGURE 10.1 March Dow Jones

1. The Reaction swing from C to D is the first Reaction swing in the new downward trend.

2. The next projected Reversal day falls between F and G. The Reaction swing of E to F is then used as the center of the Reaction cycle.

3. The Reaction swing of E to F proves to be the center of the cycle, as it projects the low at I.

reverse count from the beginning of the Reaction swing (C) back to A. This count equals 14 days. The forward count of 14 days predicts a Reversal date for Monday, February 21. This date happens to be a holiday and all the markets are closed. However, the market does not reverse on the next trading day but instead continues the downward trend. I would not have been a buyer on this day as no reversal patterns have formed. In fact, the Dow confirms a continuation pattern when it trades below the previous day's low on the trail day and closes lower than the opening price.

Using the Reaction swing of E to F, I will do a reverse count to see what kind of projection will result. The reverse count from the low at E back to the high at D equals nine days. The forward count from the high at F predicts a potential reversal on February 25 (G). The projection proves to be right on the button, as the Dow begins a five-day rally on this very date.

This is where some traders get confused because the Reversal date projected from the reverse count of C to A did not fall exactly inside a Reaction swing. In all the previous examples the Reversal dates were inside a Reaction swing; this helped to identify which swing to use for the next count. In a perfect world, this would occur every time. However, even though this Reversal date did not fall inside the Reaction swing, it is not hard to deal with. In other words, the swing of E to F becomes the center of the Reaction cycle that is used to project forward to the end of the cycle. All we do is use the closest Reaction swing (in this case the swing of E to F) as the basis for future counts. Let's see how this works.

The reverse count from the low at E back to the high at B equals 20 days. The forward count of 20 days from the high at F projects the Reversal date of March 14 (I) to be the end of the cycle.

After breaking out of the E to F Reaction swing, the Dow traded sharply lower. The bearish trend ended on March 14 (I), right on the predicted date. On the trail day, the Dow traded above the high of the Reversal date to trigger a quick 700-point rally.

The Dow Jones example is a good illustration of a market that didn't follow the cycle precisely, but still gave a trader all the information needed to predetermine potential Reversal dates. Not all markets will conform to the rules exactly. However, with practice you will be able to find the patterns. The patterns are there, just waiting to be uncovered.

One thing you will find (if you have not already come to this conclusion) is the Reaction cycle is very evident in strongly trending markets. When a market goes into a sideways range, the Reversal dates become harder to find—but they are there. You should keep in mind that the fastest and largest profits are made in the more strongly trading markets. Therefore, you have to decide which type of market you want to trade and the amount of risk you are willing to take in order to achieve the desired results.

August Bellies

For many years, one of the favorite markets for hard-core traders and risk takers was the Pork Bellies. As the trading was always fast and furious, it offered quick riches or a quick trip to the poorhouse. This spawned many stories in books and movies about the wild and crazy commodity traders. As a broker and trader, I am often asked the question, "Is there really such a thing as Pork Bellies, and if so, what are they?" I always give the standard answer, "Yes, they are where your bacon comes from, and it is a very wild market with high risk and the potential for high return." Throughout my years in this business, I have seen many traders attempt to conquer the Pork Bellies market. In the past, it was a favorite of day traders because of the high volatility and large daily trading ranges. Although in the past few years it has lost much of its volume to the stock indexes, it still offers great opportunities for traders who can identify its signals.

In August 1999, the Bellies offered one of these opportunities that was outlined almost perfectly by a Reaction cycle, with only one exception. That is why I wanted to include Figure 10.2 in this book.

On May 10, the August Bellies peaked at 61.00 (B). This date just hap-

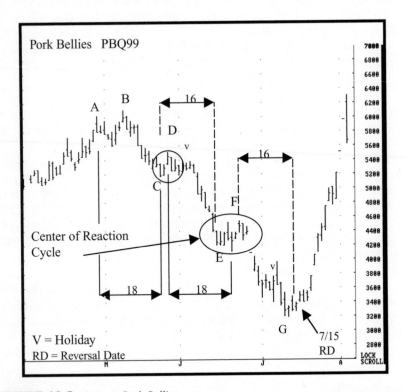

FIGURE 10.2 August Pork Bellies

1. The Pork Bellies peak at B. The first Reaction swing forms from C to D. The Reaction swing of C to D is used to determine the Reversal date that falls inside the Reaction swing of E to F.

2. The Reaction swing of E to F is used to project a Reversal date at July 15.

3. The Pork Bellies reverse on July 15 (G). However, the market continues to rally and never trades below the low at G. The downward trend has ended sooner than projected.

pened to be a Reversal date. As this was a predetermined Reversal date, a sell signal was triggered when the market traded below the low of 59.40 (the low of the Reversal date).

This sell signal was followed by a sharp price decline over the next 10 trading days until the Bellies hit a low of 51.80 on May 24 (C). After trading higher for two days, the market posted an intermediate high on May 26 (D) before it reversed to continue the downward trend. This formed the first Reaction swing of C to D.

Using this new Reaction swing, a reverse count from C back to A equals 18 days. The forward count of 18 days from D predicts a Reversal date on June 21. This date is the center of the new Reaction swing of E to F.

Normally this Reaction swing would be the center of the Reaction cycle and should be considered the center until proven otherwise. Based on that assumption, I now initiate a reverse count from this new Reaction swing.

Starting at the low (E), the reverse count to C equals 16 days, and the count back to the high at B equals 26 days. The forward counts of 16 days and 26 days from the high at F projects future Reversal dates on July 15 and July 29.

As you can see on the Pork Bellies chart, the market did indeed fall fast and hard (to the delight of all who were short) and bottomed two days before the predetermined Reversal date of July 15. Naturally, I now thought that the market could form another Reaction swing before dropping into the next Reversal date (July 29) to end the cycle.

However, the Bellies had a different plan. They reversed on the predicted Reversal date of July 15 (a buy signal confirmed by a chart pattern) and rallied over 3,000 points in only two weeks. Based on the buy signal on the July 15 Reversal date, you should have been long and enjoyed this nice bullish run.

You are most likely asking the question, "How do I know that the market would rally here and not drop into the next Reversal date of July 29?" Good question! Fortunately, there is an answer.

Look at Figures 10.3 and 10.4 to see how the entire move unfolded. As you can see, the entire price move in Bellies from B to G was divided into three separate moves by the two Reaction swings. These three separate price moves were also fairly equal in length. I point this out because many times a major move in a market will unfold in three equal legs. This is something W. D. Gann talked about often. This is also the basis of the popular Elliott Wave Theory.

One of the strongest indications that the bear market was ending occurred when time and price came together. At this point, the Bellies began what seemed to be just another Reaction swing. However, the predicted

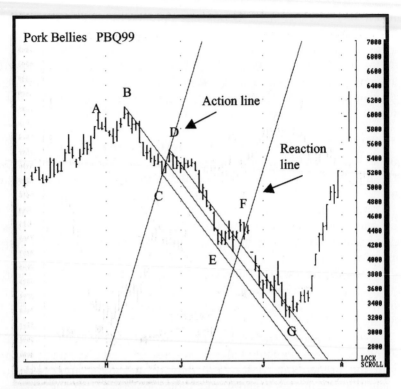

FIGURE 10.3   Action/Reaction—Three Equal Legs

1. The Action line at C to D is used to project the Reaction line that falls just underneath the Reaction swing at E to F.
2. The market trades through the Reaction line, suggesting lower prices.
3. The Action/Reaction lines identify the first two of three equal legs in the market.

Reversal date of July 15 (G) signaled a continuation of the upward price move; it did not trigger the sell signal to complete the new Reaction swing.

Figure 10.3 clearly shows the Bellies hitting the Reaction line during the projected reversal time period. The first Action line, drawn at C and D, projects a possible price move down to the mid-42.00s.

The Bellies fell right into the forecasted price range and at the Reaction line formed the Reaction swing of E to F. Using this new Reaction swing, you can project the next price target (Figure 10.4). Using the high at D and the new Reaction swing of E to F, you can project the possibility of the Bellies trading down to 32.00. The low of 31.90 proves to be the bottom. Two days later, the new bull market is confirmed by the Reversal

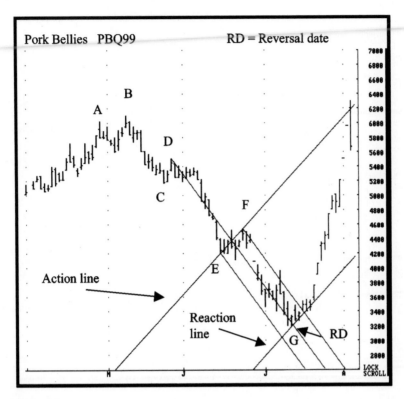

FIGURE 10.4 Action/Reaction Lines

1. From the new Action line at E to F, August Pork Bellies trade lower for 14 days to a low of 31.90, right on the Reaction line. This proves to be the bottom in the Bellies.

2. Two days later, the new bull market is confirmed by the Reversal date, triggering a buy signal.

date, triggering a buy signal. *This is a classic example of time, price, and pattern working together in harmony with the markets.*

March S&P

I want to show you one more example before we move on. Figure 10.5 is interesting because the March S&P provides a classic textbook example of the Reaction cycle. In this example, the S&P hits a major high on the predicted Reversal date to end the Reaction cycle; but it does not touch the Reaction line until two weeks later, as shown on Figure 10.6. In this case, I would trade the Reversal date sell signal because (as mentioned earlier)

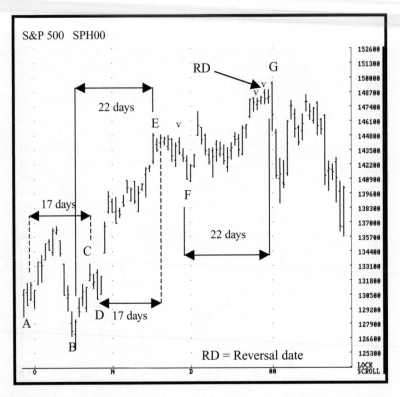

FIGURE 10.5 March S&P

1. The Reaction swing of E to F is the center of the Reaction cycle.
2. The reverse count from E to B equals 22 days.
3. The forward count of 22 days from the low at F projects a Reversal day at G.

time leads price. In other words, when the Reaction cycle says the time is up, the move is over.

In some instances, such as this one in the March S&P, the market will trade sideways until it hits the Reaction line. Figures 10.5 and 10.6 illustrate this point.

In Figure 10.5, the March S&P bottoms on October 15 (B) with a low close of 1273.00. This begins a new rally. The first Reaction swing forms from C to D. The reverse count of 17 days forecasts the market to trade higher into November 18 (E).

Right on cue, the S&P peaks at 1449.00 on the predicted date of November 18 (E) and then it begins the expected market correction. This correction forms a new Reaction swing of E to F. After posting a low on November 30, the S&P resumes the bull market into the next Reversal date.

Knowing that the Reaction swing of E to F is also the center of the Reaction cycle, proceed with the reverse count from the high at E back to the low at B. This equals 22 days. I now know with a high degree of confidence that the S&P should continue the upward trend for 22 days from the low at F until it reaches the Reversal date on December 31 (G).

Take a look at the price projections using the Action/Reaction lines as seen on Figure 10.6. See how the Reaction swing of E to F begins right on the Reaction line. This is exactly the point where time and price was working in harmony.

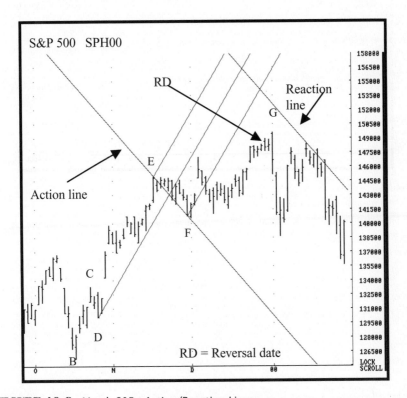

FIGURE 10.6 March S&P—Action/Reaction Lines

1. The March S&P reverses on the projected Reversal date and trades sharply lower for three days.

2. The March S&P does not hit the Reaction line on the projected Reversal date.

3. The March S&P stages a secondary rally that is turned back by the Reaction line. From this point, the S&P trades lower for the next five weeks.

The S&P continues the bullish trend for the next 22 trading days before it hits a major high one trading day after the predicted Reversal date. (On December 31, all the markets were closed; therefore, the next trading date is used for the Reversal date.)

As you can see in Figure 10.6, the S&P did turn on the projected Reversal date, but it did not reach the price objective. Don't be disheartened because all three factors—time, price, and pattern—did not converge exactly in the same place. There was still enough evidence to confirm the end of a Reaction cycle and the possible beginning of a new trend. The interesting thing about this S&P chart is you can see how the market traded sharply lower after the Reversal date sell and then rebounded just as quickly until it made contact with the Reaction line. At the Reaction line the S&P finally gave up and traded lower for the next five weeks.

CHAPTER 11

Bullish
and Bearish
Divergence

In the early 1980s, an advertisement ran in many of the financial newspapers and commodity magazines. The advertisement displayed several chart examples of markets making large price moves from major bottoms or tops. At the top of the ad and in big bold letters the caption read, "PEPS DOES IT AGAIN!" The ad suggested that if you would learn this secret, you could determine Precise Entry Points (PEPS) that would allow you to enter the market at or near the major top or bottom of any market.

The selling price of the PEPS system started at $1,000, but quickly rose to $1,200 as sales increased. Before long the system sold for $1,500. (I don't think it went much higher.) It was an impressive ad campaign that made you believe this was to be a great discovery and the way to instant wealth.

One day while I was sitting in my office a good friend and fellow trader walked in with great excitement about a new purchase. Yup, that's right! He had just paid $1,200 for the PEPS trading method. He laid out his charts before me and proceeded to describe the secret indicator. Excitedly he said, "All you have to do is watch this indicator. When the price makes a new high but the indicator does not make a new high, it means the market is ready to top. The secret is to wait until this occurs three times and then you sell the market."

"Bob," I said, "isn't that secret indicator simply a slow stochastic? So, the secret is to wait for price of the commodity to make a new high and then when the slow stochastic does not do the same three times, you sell,

147

right? Bob, you have just bought a very expensive manual about bullish and bearish divergence!"

Unlike Bob, you don't have to pay the $1,200, because I'm going to teach you about bullish and bearish divergence. It can be a great tool to use in conjunction with Reversal dates.

One of the exciting things about bullish and bearish divergence is it can be used in different time frames. I have used it on weekly charts and on shorter time frames all the way down to five-minute charts.

The slow stochastics technical oscillator (SSTO) is based on the theory that, as prices move higher, the daily close should increasingly reflect the high of the daily range. Likewise, as prices decrease, the daily close tends to become closer to the low of the daily range.

SSTO calculations are based on the rate of change in the daily high, low, and close. The SSTO chart needs two lines and three values. The three values are: the raw value, %K, and %D. These values are plotted on a scale of 0 to 100. When the raw value and the %K are plotted on the same chart, the result is a "fast stochastic." The fast stochastic shows you many up and down swings in a very short time period. When the %K and %D are plotted together you have a "slow stochastic" that smooths out the data.

I'm not going to describe the formula for the SSTO because it is available on most technical charting software. Even though you do not have to calculate the formula, you will have to decide the number of time periods to use. The lower the number of periods used, the more swings in the SSTO and therefore the more signals. A higher number of time periods will smooth the indicator and generate fewer signals.

The miracle system I mentioned earlier used nine days as its parameter. I prefer 20 days because I believe it generates better trading signals for the longer-term trend changes. As everybody has his or her own preferences, you should test different time periods to see which one matches your trading style.

USING THE SSTO AS A TIMING INDICATOR

There are many different ways to trade using the SSTO, but there is only one way I like to use it, and that is when the market is showing either a bullish or bearish divergence in conjunction with a projected Reversal date.

A bullish divergence is created when a market makes a new low, but the SSTO does not make a new low.

The strongest signals occur after the market has repeated this pattern two to three times. The following chart examples illustrate this concept very well.

Let's look at a few examples of bullish and bearish divergence using the slow stochastic.

Cattle

As shown in Figure 11.1, during the latter part of 2000 and early in 2001 the Cattle made three consecutive new highs within a five-week period. In the same time period, the SSTO revealed weakness in the market (even as the Cattle traded to new highs) when the SSTO made three lower highs in the same time frame.

On January 16, the Cattle reached the third peak but were unable to

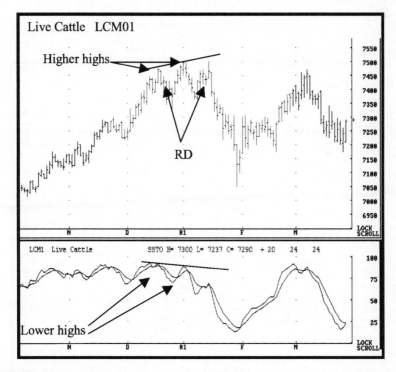

FIGURE 11.1 Bearish Divergence in June Cattle

1. June Cattle prices make three consecutive new higher highs. During the same time period, the SSTO makes three consecutive lower highs, forming a bearish divergence.

2. The June Cattle top out after the third new high, and a major price decline follows.

continue higher due to the underlying weakness. This peak was followed by a sharp price collapse over the next two and a half weeks. The SSTO bearish divergence gave warning of this bull market demise several days before the end. If you had read the warning signs, you would have been prepared for the turn in the Cattle market.

Soybeans

The Soybeans (shown in Figure 11.2) made a new contract low on July 17. The SSTO was already showing signs of strength in the Soybeans, as the SSTO had made a low higher than the previous low just days earlier.

The Soybeans made a weak attempt at a rally and then retested the contract low. At the same time, the SSTO made yet another higher low. The bullish divergence ended the downward trend in the Soybeans, as the double bottom held and the Soybeans rallied for four weeks.

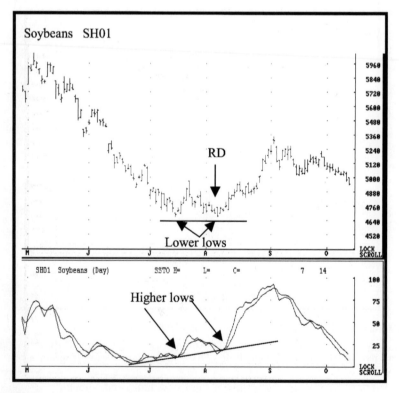

FIGURE 11.2   Bullish Divergence in March Soybeans

Natural Gas

During the winter of 2000, the Natural Gas staged a massive rally that was caused by supply shortages and delivery problems (see Figure 11.3). The N-Gas formed three consecutive higher highs. However, the SSTO began to signal an end to the rally, as it made lower highs during the same time period. On January 9, the bullish market came to a sudden end and N-Gas prices fell as fast as they had rallied.

Dow Jones

This is the market that was expected to rally forever (see Figure 11.4). While the television experts were preaching 12,000, the SSTO was saying, "No way!" When the Dow was making new highs in late December and early January, the SSTO was showing weakness, as it was making lower highs. This was a great big red flag warning that the rally was coming to an

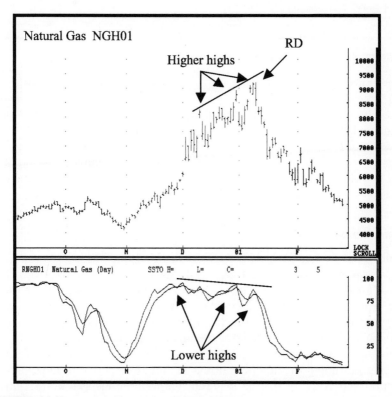

FIGURE 11.3 Bearish Divergence in March N-Gas

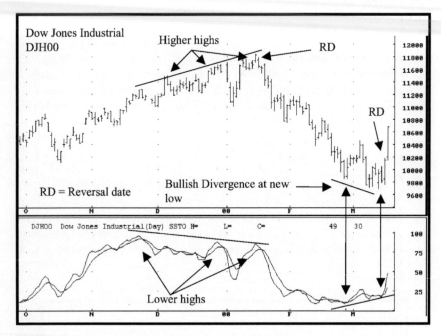

FIGURE 11.4   Bearish Divergence in March Dow Jones

end. Finally, on January 14, a predicted Reversal day, it ended. The Dow made its last new high and collapsed from exhaustion.

Looking at the chart example, you can see new bullish divergence starting to build as the Dow makes new lows. All the major highs and lows just shown gave warning signs long before they happened. All you have to do is be aware and listen to the market.

June Nasdaq 100

While the Dow Jones began to show weakness during December and January, the Nasdaq 100 was still on a roll (see Figure 11.5). When the Dow Jones finally reversed and began to trade lower during January, the Nasdaq 100 broke through overhead resistance and reached a new all-time high, making the statement, "High tech is king." This powerful trend continued into early March until the Nasdaq 100 finally peaked on March 9, 2000.

After making a three-day correction, the Nasdaq 100 roared back, quickly pushing past the old contract high and surging to a new all-time high on March 23, 2000. This inspired renewed enthusiasm in the "sky is the limit" investment camp—but it was not to be.

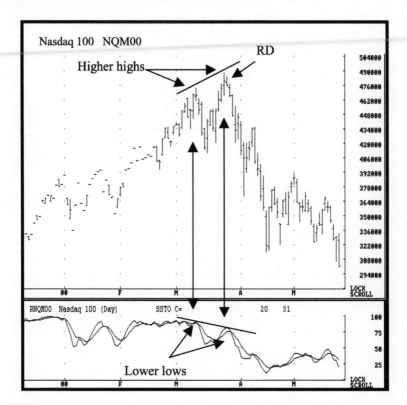

FIGURE 11.5   Bearish Divergence in Nasdaq 100

During this time, while the Nasdaq 100 was roaring higher and fueling the buying frenzy, it was also becoming very tired and was nearing exhaustion. The market tried to warn investors and traders that it was nearing the end of the race—it had the finish line in its sights and it was going to give one last surge before it exhausted itself. The signs were there; but you had to see them and know how to interpret them.

The Nasdaq 100 made two consecutive new highs, but the SSTO was beginning to fail. As the market was making new highs, the SSTO was making two consecutive lower highs. Finally, the SSTO turned south and the Nasdaq 100 did as well, falling sharply over the next two weeks.

CHAPTER 12

When You Can't Find the Cycle

This next statement will be very disappointing for many of you: Unfortunately, you will not be able to find the beginning of a Reaction cycle every time you want to trade a market. In this event, what do you do? Can you still use the Reversal dates for timing? Fortunately, yes, you can.

When I cannot find, to my satisfaction, what I believe to be the beginning of a Reaction cycle in a market, I will identify a Reaction swing and use it to determine future Reversal dates by simply extending both the reverse and forward counts.

I like to describe Reversal dates as being similar to dropping a pebble into a pool of water. The ripples travel equally in all directions. If you identify the correct Reaction swing, it will act the same way in the markets.

April Cattle

To illustrate this concept, we will revisit a market used earlier in this book—the April Cattle. See Figure 12.1. Can you see the ripples seeming to flow equally in both directions?

Instead of starting at the beginning of the Reaction cycle (B), we will go right to the Reaction swing marked E to F. Using this Reaction swing as a starting point, we perform a reverse count from the high at E. (This reverse count is done in the same manner as the previous reverse counts.) The reverse counts to the previous Reaction swings equal 15 days, 20 days, 24 days, and 38 days. With this information, we can estimate future Reversal dates. Count forward from the end of the Reaction

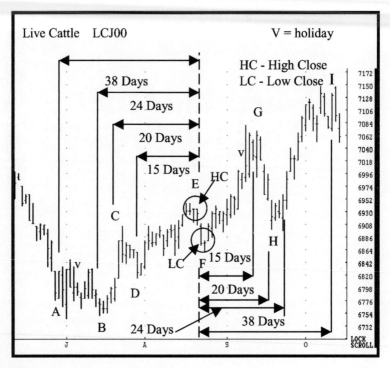

FIGURE 12.1 Extending the Count

1. The Reaction swing of E to F is used as the center point.
2. The reverse count to D projects the high at G.
3. The reverse count to C and B confirms the low at H.
4. The reverse count to A predicts the major high at I.

swing (F). This projects potential Reversal dates 15, 20, 24, and 38 days into the future. The chart illustrates this point very well. Each predetermined Reversal date falls on a corresponding swing in the market. The timing of each market reversal was accurately predicted several days before it actually occurred.

September Crude Oil

The next pattern we'll look at occurred in the September Crude Oil (Figure 12.2). Instead of looking for the beginning of the Reaction cycle, we can see that a Reaction swing has just been confirmed at E to F. This is a quick way to determine Reversal dates once the trend is already under

FIGURE 12.2 Extending the Count from Reaction Swing
1. The reverse count is extended back from the high of the Reaction swing (E).
2. The reverse count from E of 16, 19, and 28 days projects possible Reversal dates on day 16 (G), 19 (H), and 28 (I).

way. We simply count back from E and end up with a reverse count of 16, 19, and 28 days. Counting forward from the end of the Reaction swing (F), we now project potential Reversal dates on June 14 (G), June 19 (H), and June 30 (I).

The September Crude Oil trades out of the Reaction swing at E to F but goes into a sideways trading pattern. Three days before the predicted Reversal date (G), Crude Oil jumps out of this consolidation pattern and trades higher, before it tops on June 14 (G). Three days later, after falling over 200 points, the Crude reverses on the next predicted Reversal date, June 19 (H).

Crude continues the bullish trend until June 30 (I), where it finally has exhausted all buying and turns lower.

June S&P 500

Here is one more example before moving on, this time using the S&P 500 (Figure 12.3). The Reaction swing in this example is marked as A to B. We perform the reverse count from the low at A. The reverse counts to the highs and lows of previous Reaction swings are marked on the chart as 10, 14, 16, 20, and 26.

In this example, the reverse count is continued further back than in any of the earlier examples in order to show how the reverse count can be continued back until the beginning of the contract. However, I usually like to stop before the Reaction swings become hard to identify.

As you can see, the accuracy of the reversals does not weaken as we

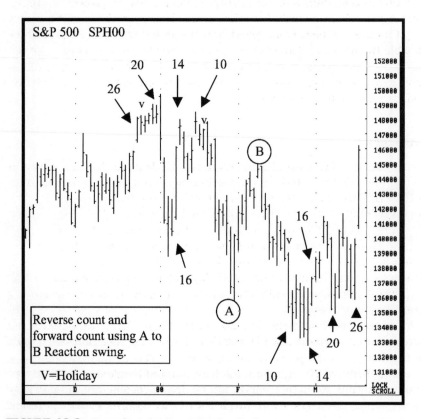

FIGURE 12.3 Extending the Count Further Back

1. The Reaction swing marked A to B is used for the reverse and forward counts.

2. The reverse count is extended beyond the first Reaction swing. The day count for each pivot swing is marked during the reverse count.

3. The corresponding dates are marked on the forward count.

extend the length of the reverse count. Counting forward from B, the S&P posts a low on the 10th day that is followed by a slight bounce and another significant low on the 14th day. Day 16 is a continuation pattern that just happens to fall in the exact center of this upward thrust. On the 20th day, a reversal occurs to push the S&P sharply higher over the next two days. The market then falls back into day 26 before it reverses and trades higher. Are you beginning to get the picture?

USING A NEW REACTION SWING

The previous examples in this chapter illustrate how to project future Reversal dates from a single Reaction swing. However, this is not the only way that this can be accomplished. You are probably beginning to see how flexible the Reversal date concept can be. The next few examples use different swings to project future Reversal dates. In other words, every time a new Reaction swing forms, it can be used to project the next Reaction swing. Let's see how it works.

Soybeans

Using the July Soybeans (Figure 12.4), we will begin at the first Reaction swing, identified as C to D. From the low at C, count back to the contract high at B. This equals 13 days. Next, count forward from the high (D). The forward count of 13 days falls right on the lowest close (E) before a short-term rally occurs. This rally forms a new Reaction swing of E to F.

Now proceed with a new reverse count from the low of this new Reaction swing (E) back to the low close at C. This count equals 15 days. The subsequent forward count of 15 days again falls on a significant low (G). Another short-term rally follows and forms the next Reaction swing of G to H.

Continuing on with the July Soybeans (Figure 12.5), we perform the reverse count from the low marked G of this newest Reaction swing back to the low (E) of the previous Reaction swing. This count equals 20 days. Counting forward 20 days from the high marked H takes us down to yet another low at I. From this market low (I), the Soybeans stage a small rally over the next five days before turning lower to confirm another Reaction swing (I to J).

I know this example seems like it has gone on forever, but I want to see it through until the end (the end is near).

Using the new Reaction swing of I to J, the reverse count back to the low of the previous Reaction swing equals five days. When the market

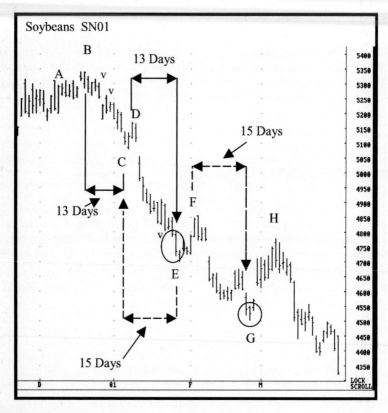

FIGURE 12.4 Using a New Reaction Swing—Soybeans I

1. The Reaction swing of C to D is used to determine the next Reaction swing of E to F.

2. The reverse count from C back to the high of B equals 13 days. The forward count from D to the low at E equals 13 days.

3. This Reversal date (E) is the beginning of a new Reaction swing.

reaches day 5 of the forward count, the Soybeans are trading at the support provided by the previous low (I). To many traders, this would appear to be a double bottom forming, but the price pattern does not confirm a bottom; instead, it indicates that a possible new low could be expected.

The very next day, Soybeans fall through the support and trade to a new contract low. As there is not a new Reaction swing to use, we continue the reverse count back to the previous Reaction swing (Y) (this count equals 10 days). Counting forward 10 days from the high of the Reaction swing (J) projects April 25 (K) as the next Reversal date.

Finally, after using four different Reaction swings to project future swings (as shown in Figure 12.6), the downward trend in the July Soy-

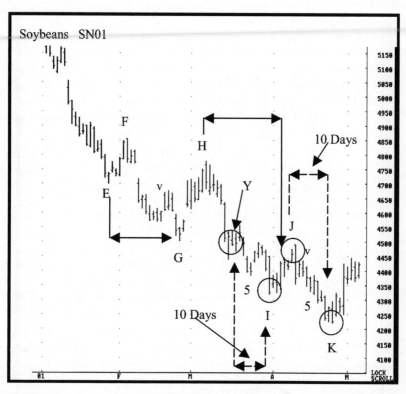

FIGURE 12.5 Using a New Reaction Swing—Soybeans II

1. The Reaction swing of G to H is used to determine the beginning of the Reaction swing of I to J.

2. The reverse count from I to the low Y of a small Reaction swing equals five days. This identifies a continuation pattern in the forward count.

3. The reverse count from I to Y equals 10 days. A 10-day forward count identified the major low at K.

beans comes to an end, exactly on the Reversal date forecasted by the last Reaction swing. This is a good example of the flexibility of the Reversal date indicator. Each Reaction swing in the market was identified days in advance. *When used properly, every trader could use this indicator with any type of trading approach. Because in trading, timing is everything.*

August Pork Bellies

If the preceding example didn't excite you, wait until you see this one using charts of the August Pork Bellies. Throughout the years, aggressive

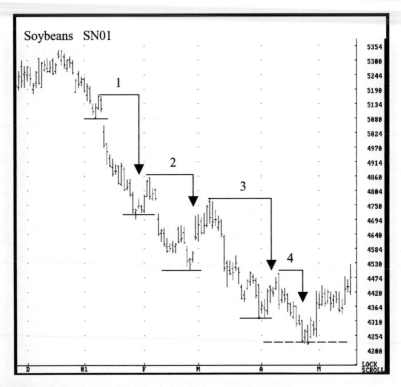

FIGURE 12.6 Using a New Reaction Swing—Soybeans III

1. The first Reaction swing (1) is used to identify the time for the second Reaction swing (2).

2. The second Reaction swing (2) is used to identify the time for the third Reaction swing (3).

3. The third Reaction swing (3) is used to identify the time for the fourth Reaction swing (4).

4. The fourth Reaction swing (4) is used to identify the time of the exact major low.

traders have always tried to conquer the Bellies. The volatility in the Bellies has made for a difficult market to trade. But I think this example will demonstrate how a little help with timing could have given many of these traders an edge.

We'll start with the Reaction swing of C to D in Figure 12.7. The Bellies peak at B 10 days before trading to the low close at C. This low close is followed by a two-day retracement to D before the Bellies head into a pennant formation. It takes seven days before the Bellies trade low enough to break through support and continue the downward trend.

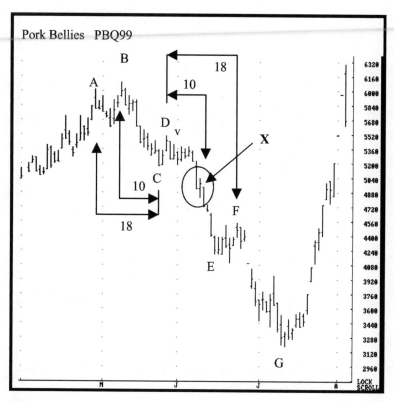

FIGURE 12.7 Using a New Reaction Swing—Pork Bellies I

1. The Reaction swing of C to D is used to identify a continuation pattern marked X and the new Reaction swing of E to F.

2. When a projected Reversal date confirms a continuation pattern (X) instead of a reversal pattern, the continuation pattern usually falls in the center of the price move.

Once the support is broken, the Reaction swing is completed and the reverse count can begin.

The count from C back to B equals 10 days. A forward count of 10 days from the high (D) has the next Reversal date falling on June 9 (X). On this projected Reversal date, the market trades lower than the previous day's low and closes at the low of the day. The following day, the trail day, is a narrow range day and also closes lower than the opening price. We now know that this type of price pattern suggests a possible continuation of the downward slide. This also offers a very good clue as to how many more days there are before the next potential Reversal day. Here is what I mean.

Take a look at the Reversal date marked X. The count back to the high of the previous Reaction swing (D) equals 11 days. Now, starting at X, count forward 11 days. The 11th day is another Reversal date (F), and the beginning of another bearish leg in the Bellies.

When a projected Reversal date does not confirm a reversal pattern, it can be a continuation pattern. This type of pattern will usually appear in the center of the price move. This is just one more way to help confirm future Reversal dates.

Before moving on, let's go back to the Reaction swing of C to D and continue the reverse count that we began earlier. You see, now that we know the count back to B provided the date for a *continuation* pattern, we can do one of two things (or both if we wish). We can use the Reversal date (X) as the center on this price move (as just illustrated) or we can continue the reverse count back to the high marked A. This count equals 18 days.

In Figure 12.8, the forward count of 18 days falls inside the Reaction

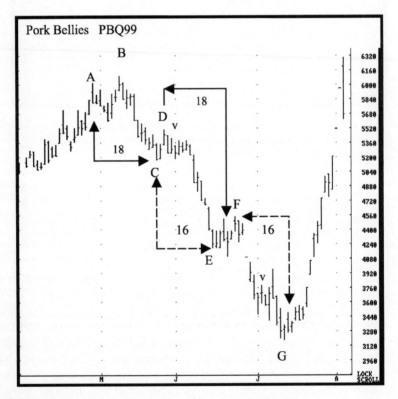

FIGURE 12.8   Using a New Reaction Swing—Pork Bellies II

swing of E to F. Notice how both methods of measurement take you to the same Reaction swing. (The other was shown in Figure 12.7.)

Using the new Reaction swing of E to F, the reverse count to C equals 16 days. The 16-day forward count from F lands right on the major low at G.

Even though I have gone into great detail describing these two alternative methods of determining future Reversal dates, I have not shown how the Action/Reaction lines fall into place with these methods. The next two chart examples illustrate how the Action/Reaction lines work in conjunction with this new method of counting.

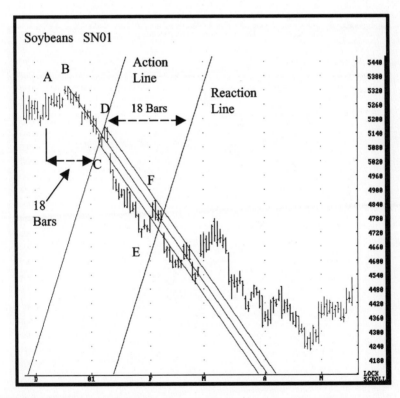

FIGURE 12.9 Action/Reaction Lines on New Reaction Swings—Soybeans I

1. The Action line is drawn through the Reaction swing of C to D.

2. The reverse count from C to A is 18 bars. The center line is marked 18 bars forward from D and the Reaction line is drawn at E to F.

3. The new Reaction swing of E to F climbs right along the Reaction line.

APPLYING ACTION/REACTION LINES TO THE NEW REACTION SWINGS

The previous examples in this chapter all demonstrated how time can be identified using Reaction swing forward and reverse counts. The addition of a price confirmation would be frosting on the cake.

You probably know by now that the best way to show this technique is through numerous chart examples. To determine the price is as simple as using each consecutive Reaction swing to determine the next Reaction swing.

When the Reaction swing has been identified, just follow the guidelines for overlaying the Action/Reaction lines and then see what happens. Figures 12.9 to 12.13 show how it is done.

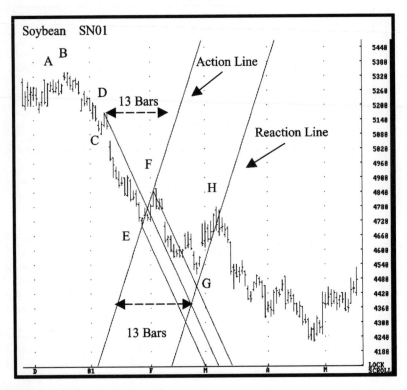

FIGURE 12.10   Action/Reaction Lines on New Reaction Swings—Soybeans II

1. A new Action line is drawn through the Reaction swing of E to F. The reverse count from E to C is 13 bars.

2. The center line is marked 13 bars forward from the high at F. The Reaction line is drawn. The Reaction swing of G to H climbs right up the Reaction line.

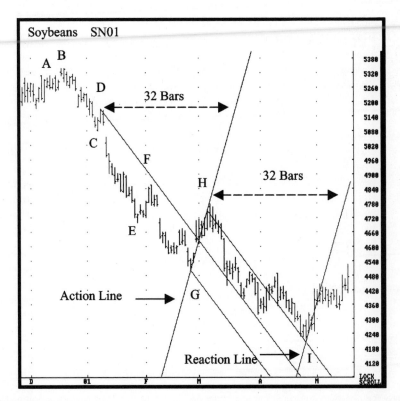

FIGURE 12.11 Action/Reaction Lines on New Reaction Swings—Soybeans III

1. The Action/Reaction lines are now applied to the new Reaction swing of G to H. The reverse count is 32 bars.

2. The center line is marked 32 bars forward from H and the Reaction line is drawn.

3. The Soybeans hit the Reaction line on the projected Reversal date at I. The Reversal date and the Reaction line connect at a major low.

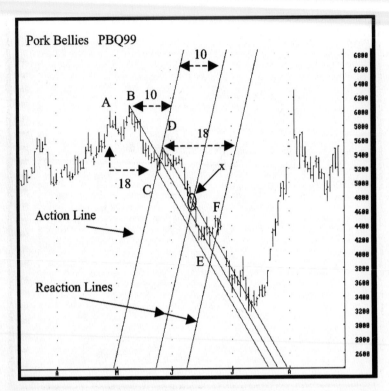

FIGURE 12.12 Action/Reaction Lines on New Reaction Swings—Pork Bellies I

1. The reverse count, from C to B and then to A, equals 10 bars and then 8 bars for a total of 18 bars. The forward count of 10 bars falls in the center of the price move marked X.

2. When the price closes through the X Reaction line, it indicates a continuation of a price move into the next Reaction line.

3. The center line is marked 18 bars forward from D and the next Reaction line is drawn. Bellies trade higher as soon as the market reaches this Reaction line to form the Reaction swing of E to F.

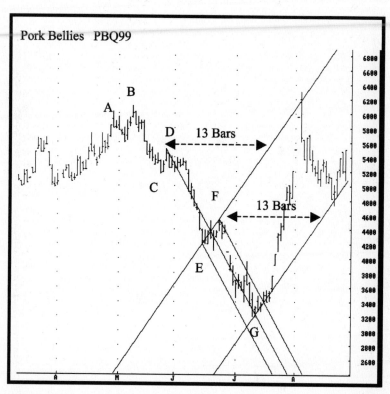

FIGURE 12.13 Action/Reaction Lines on New Reaction Swings—Pork Bellies II

1. Using the low of the Reaction swing marked E to F, the reverse count equals 13 bars.

2. The center line is marked 13 bars forward from F and the Reaction line is drawn.

3. The Pork Bellies find strong support at the Reaction line and reverse on the predicted Reversal date. This signal ends a prolonged price decline and marks the beginning of a sharp rally.

CHAPTER 13

Long-Term Trend versus Short-Term Trend

"The trend is your friend." We've all heard this saying hundreds of times; but it still remains one of the hardest strategies for a trader to follow. When will the trend end? How long will it last? How far will it go? These questions, and many more, plague all traders. Even though I don't have the ultimate secret formula, I am going to show you something that will go a long way in helping you determine the length, strength, and longevity of a trend.

By now you are well versed on the Reaction cycle and its significance to market behavior. Some of you may even be vaguely aware of its similarity to the Elliott Wave Theory. Even though they're similar (they are both based on the concept of natural cycles in the markets), I believe that the Reaction cycle is much easier to identify and implement.

A-B-C PATTERN

The Elliott Wave Theory suggests that a market trend should unfold in five identifiable waves. Each price move in the direction of the prevailing, dominant trend is followed by a price retracement. Once the market has completed the fifth and final wave, the market will experience a substantial price correction that consists of three waves. These three waves are identified as A-B-C.

The concept of the A-B-C correction can also be applied to the Reaction cycle. The presence of the A-B-C correction is a very important indicator of things to follow. Earlier, there were several examples of the Reaction cycle that took you from the beginning through to the end. Some of these examples went from a bearish Reaction cycle directly into a bullish cycle, or vice versa. In these instances the Reaction cycles all had one thing in common—they were short-term trends. There is nothing wrong with trading short-term trends; in fact, most traders prefer to trade on a short-term basis. However, if there were a reliable way to identify when a market was in a longer-term trend, it would definitely benefit the trader. "The trend is your friend." If you can avoid fighting the trend, your life becomes much easier. If I have a choice between swimming against the current or with it, I will choose swimming with the current; it is much easier and a person can survive much longer.

After a market has completed a bullish Reaction cycle, it will do one of two things. Either it will reverse and begin a new bearish Reaction cycle (this will be revealed soon enough as the price pattern unfolds) or the market will form an A-B-C pattern and begin a new bullish Reaction cycle. In other words, the A-B-C pattern is just a pause inside the longer-term trend.

There are two important characteristics of this pattern. First, the pattern will contain a small Reaction swing in the center of a larger one. This small Reaction swing is what forms the A-B-C pattern, and most importantly, it will identify the *center of the A-B-C correction*. This tells you when the correction will end and the new Reaction cycle will begin. The second important characteristic of the A-B-C correction is that it will usually be in the center of the longer-term trend. Therefore, you can now use the new Reaction swing to project future Reversal dates and use the A-B-C pattern to measure price projections. This may seem confusing, but the chart examples will help illustrate how this works.

June T-Bonds

Take a look at Figure 13.1. You will recognize this market from previous examples of the Reaction cycle and Action/Reaction lines discussed in Chapters 4 and 5. As we have already gone through this example earlier, I am not going to bother you with all the reverse and forward counts. The area we will concentrate on is the Reaction swing marked E to F. This was the largest and longest-lasting Reaction swing in this long-term trend. This Reaction swing was also a gauge of things to come. In the center of this large Reaction swing is a small Reaction swing that consists of only three days; it is identified by 1 and 2.

An Elliott Wave trader would identify the price move from E to 1 as A. The small correction from 1 to 2 would be the B wave, and the price move from 2 to F would be known as the C wave—thus the name A-B-C.

The key point here is this: The Reaction swing of 1 to 2 can be used

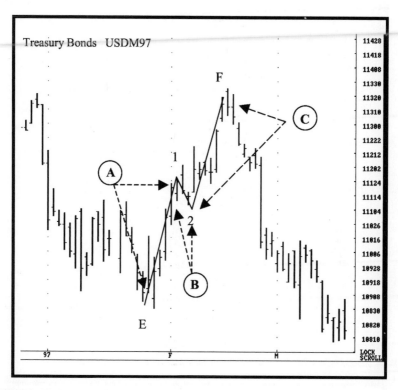

FIGURE 13.1 A-B-C Pattern

1. The price move from E to 1 is A; the price move from 1 to 2 is B; the price move from 2 to F is C.

2. The reverse count from 1 back to E is six days. The forward count from 2 to F is also six days. Therefore, the 1 to 2 Reaction swing is the center of the A-B-C pattern.

to determine the end of the Reaction swing of E to F. The reverse count from 1 to E is six days. The forward count from 2 to F is also six days. Therefore, the Reaction swing of 1 to 2 is in the exact center of the A-B-C pattern.

Let's move on to the next step of measuring the length of the potential trend. You may think that this is a rehash of Chapter 4 (see Figure 4.5). Even though it may seem very familiar, the process is for a completely different reason. Learning this A-B-C pattern will help you to identify a *new* trend or a correction *inside* a long-term trend. This pattern is one of the strongest indicators I have found. Whether you use it or not, it is important to know about it.

In Figure 13.2, the T-Bonds have just established a high at F. This

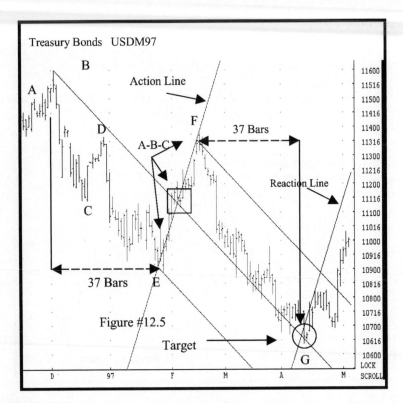

FIGURE 13.2 A-B-C Pattern—Treasury Bonds

completes the A-B-C formation and marks the beginning of a new bearish Reaction cycle. The rest is simple. Based on the theory that the A-B-C formation usually appears in the center of a long-term trend, the Action/Reaction lines are drawn; you already know this process, so let's look at the chart with the Action/Reaction lines already applied.

Using the Reaction swing of E to F (also known as the A-B-C pattern) as the Action line, the center line is drawn from the beginning of the trend (B). Once this is done, the Reaction line can be plotted. We now have a credible target price for the T-Bonds.

The Reaction line portends a target price between 107-00 and 106-10. In mid-April, the T-Bonds bottom at 106-12.

Because of the A-B-C pattern and a good understanding of market behavior, a trader can have a high degree of confidence in the direction of the trend and trade the market accordingly. Let's look at a couple more examples.

September Corn

The September Corn chart (Figure 13.3) offers a unique example of a market that collapses at the end of a long-term trend to reach the Reaction line before it turns higher.

After reversing in mid-October the Corn has been trading in a steady downtrend for several weeks. In late February, Corn begins a four-week correction, against the prevailing trend. A three-day (A-B-C) Reaction swing forms in the center of this correction. The market correction finally reaches a peak in late March and then reverses.

After the resumption of the downward trend is well underway, the Action/Reaction lines can be applied. One would assume that the trend would continue at the same rate of decline as before. This therefore projects a possible bottom near the 2.05 to 2.00 price range. However, the

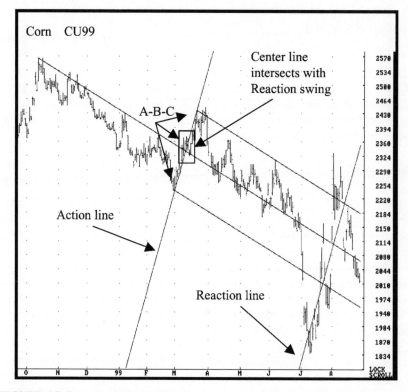

FIGURE 13.3 A-B-C Pattern—Corn

1. The A-B-C pattern identifies both the center of the longer-term trend and the center of the correction. The pattern links two separate Reaction cycles.

Corn collapses during the last two weeks of this trend as it falls all the way down to the mid-1.80s, reaching the Reaction line. Even during this extreme market drop, the Reaction line provides an accurate target and support for the very weak Corn market.

As you will notice, the larger Reaction swing of A-B-C is also the center of the longer-term trend.

Using this Reaction line as a reference point provides an excellent target for traders who are short the market or an entry point for traders waiting to buy the Corn.

FIVE-WAVE PATTERN

Just like everything else in the market, no rule is without an exception. Even though the A-B-C (three-wave) pattern is prevalent, on occasion the market will complete the entire five-wave pattern during this correction phase. Regardless, the five-wave pattern can still be used as the measuring point. I usually look for the A-B-C pattern to help identify a long-term trend; but sometimes I find more than the A-B-C.

Let's review the Elliott Wave Theory. It simply says that the market will unfold in five waves and then correct in three waves. Figures 13.2 and 13.3 illustrated the three-wave (A-B-C) concept. Occasionally, all five waves will be completed during the Reaction swing correction. Figure 13.4 illustrates this five-wave pattern.

August Crude Oil

August Crude Oil bottoms in late December and then begins to climb steadily higher over the next 36 trading days; this completes the Reaction cycle. When the market hits the end of the cycle, the timing is right for a correction.

The price correction pulls the market lower and it retraces over 60 percent of the upward move. The Crude finally finds support inside this 60 percent buy window.

Now let's look at Figure 13.5, which shows the five-wave pattern formed inside this A-B-C price correction. The previous two examples (Corn and T-Bonds) both had identifiable A-B-C patterns that were visible inside the corrections. However, here the market unfolds in a five-wave pattern. Regardless, the large Reaction swing of 1 to 2 in the center of the A-B-C pattern still is used to project the low of wave C on April 4.

Here is how it works. The large Reaction swing in the center of this

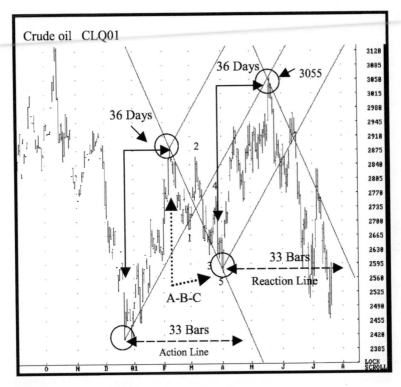

FIGURE 13.4 A-B-C Pattern with Five-Wave Pattern

1. Inside the larger A-B-C pattern is a smaller five-wave pattern.

2. Even though the C wave of the A-B-C pattern contains a small Reaction swing, the larger Reaction swing can be used to easily identify the A-B-C pattern.

3. The center line passes through the middle of the larger swing pattern, also helping identify it as an A-B-C pattern.

pattern is considered the B wave. It is used in the same way as any other Reaction swing. Beginning at the low, reverse count to the high at the beginning of the A wave. This reverse count equals 14 days. (Remember to account for the President's Day holiday.) However, this time the forward count of 14 days does not mark the end of the price move. Instead it falls on a high swing, which gives an indication of the next possible move. Since the market was trading higher as it entered this Reversal date (14), we can assume the market is ready to reverse and trade lower once again. Therefore, continue the Reverse count from the high (marked 14) on back to the high of the previous Reaction swing. This count equals 18 days. Day 18 of the forward count marks the end of the A-B-C correction and the resumption of the bullish trend. Even though this pattern may not be picture-

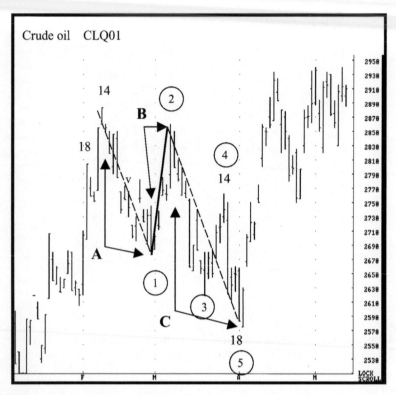

FIGURE 13.5   Inside the A-B-C Pattern

perfect, it still provides the necessary information to determine the duration of the following leg in the bull market.

Once the bullish trend is reestablished, the Action/Reaction lines are applied. The reverse count equals 33 bars. Once we have counted forward 33 bars, we can mark the Reaction line on the center line, projecting the possible price target where the long-term trend should end. In this case, the August Crude Oil hits its high point at 30.55, after reaching the Reaction line (as illustrated in Figure 13.4).

CHAPTER 14

When Is the Price Right?

I have spent a great amount of time talking about time and price, with a heavy emphasis on time. This is because time is usually the most important factor of market behavior. However, sometimes the market is influenced by unexpected outside factors. This can catch the markets by surprise and cause extreme movements in price. This type of market action offers golden opportunities for traders if they are prepared and know how to react.

Explosive price moves have always been a cause of stress and anxiety for traders. This is where the two human emotions of fear and greed really come into play. Greed causes the trader to hang on to a position too long in the hope that the extreme price movement will continue. Fear hampers others as they exit too early and miss much of the price move.

ACTION/REACTION LINES

Having confidence in predetermined price targets will help alleviate these overpowering emotions. Action/Reaction lines will help to determine these price targets. As soon as a Reaction swing has been identified, the Action/Reaction lines should be applied. If the market makes an unexpected and spectacular price move, the Action/Reaction lines will give you a reference point to determine where and when to exit the position. Let's look at some examples to illustrate this point.

April Gold

April Gold (shown in Figure 14.1) bottomed in early December 2001 (A). From this major low, the Gold traded higher into mid-January (B). At B, the market made a two-week correction into the buy window. Once this price correction was over, the Gold resumed the upward trend to confirm a new Reaction swing of B to C. As soon as you determine this as a Reaction swing, draw the Action/Reaction lines to project a target price and a future line of resistance.

A reverse count followed by a forward count will help to determine the next Reversal date. A reverse count from B to A equals 23 days (in-

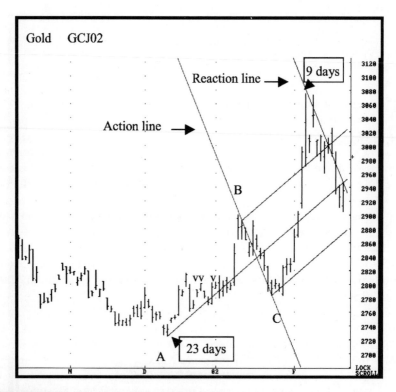

FIGURE 14.1 When Is the Price Right? Gold

1. A reverse count from B back to A suggests that the Gold should reach the Reaction line in 23 days.

2. Due to unforeseen outside influence, Gold reaches the Reaction line in nine days. This provides a large profit in a short-time period.

3. When a market reaches the Reaction line quicker than expected, it will usually retrace to meet the center line on the Reversal date.

clude three days in the count for holidays). Thus, the Gold should gradually trade higher for 23 days until it hits the Reaction line.

Without warning, though, Argentina came to the brink of financial collapse. Their president resigned and the country was thrown into chaos. Panic intensified, as there was fear of the crisis spreading to neighboring countries. This news caused a surge in Gold prices. Instead of taking 23 days to reach the Reaction line, Gold reached the target line in nine days. The surge from 279.00 to 307.00 was one of the largest price moves that Gold had experienced in quite some time. However, the opportunity to exit near the high was short-lived. On the ninth day Gold gapped open higher; it rallied to 307.00 to hit the Reaction line and then dropped below 300.00, all in a time span of less than four hours. If a trader had been sitting back and wondering what to do, he or she would have been unable to exit when the time was right.

Although this does not happen every time the market makes an exaggerated price move, the market will usually experience a price correction or move into a sideways price range before continuing the move. By knowing this, a trader is often given the opportunity to reenter the market at a better price.

March Cocoa

During the month of September 2002, news started to filter out about problems in the cocoa-producing countries. Rumors of financial problems, lower crop yields, and even a shortage of shipping bags were hindering exports and causing concern for commercial users. As shown in Figure 14.2, Cocoa prices started to move higher from A, and the market posted some of its strongest gains in months. The first big move lasted about one month before the market began a large price correction. This correction pulled the Cocoa back into the buy window, where it established a secondary bottom and soon resumed the rally. This confirmed a new Reaction swing.

This Reaction swing could now be used to overlay the Action/Reaction line and project a Reaction line and a potential price target. The reverse count from B to A equals 17 bars. This projects a potential Reversal date that is 17 bars into the future from the low at C.

The Cocoa did not do much during the first eight days after C. Suddenly, news hit the market and caused a price surge and a new sense of urgency among traders. During the next six trading days, the Cocoa jumped from 1000 to over 1240, and hit the Reaction line. *Price has exceeded time.* This offers two options: (1) use this opportunity to take profits on all long positions, or (2) stay in the position in case Cocoa moves higher. A trader who chooses the latter scenario must move a protective stop up to protect profits in the event of a price reversal. In this example, the Cocoa

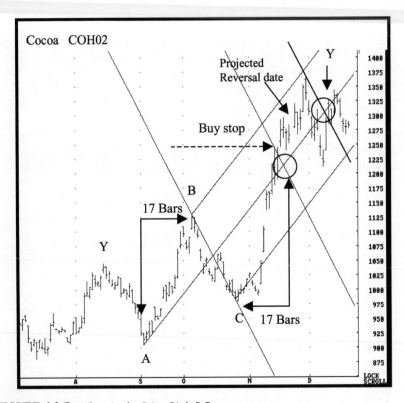

FIGURE 14.2 When Is the Price Right? Cocoa

1. Cocoa reaches the Reaction line before the Reversal date. When this happens, it is best to take profits at the Reaction line. Then place a buy stop above the high of the price bar. In this example the market continued to rally and a new long trade would be entered.

2. The Cocoa trades through the Reaction line during the following day. This portends a move to the next Reaction line.

touched the Reaction line and then fell back for the remainder of the trading session. However, the correction was short-lived as the market rallied the very next day.

A good way to handle this type of market situation is to exit the position at the Reaction line. This assures a good exit price. Then place a buy stop above the high and let it sit in place for two to three days. This assures an entry if the market continues through the Reaction line. Once the market closes above the initial Reaction line, draw another Reaction line to determine the next price target.

In this example, the count continues through to Y. Use this information to draw the next Reaction line. The Cocoa rallied through the initial Reaction line to initiate a new long position. The Cocoa then traded right up to the next Reaction line.

December S&P 500—Five-Minute Chart

The five-minute chart of the December S&P 500 (Figure 14.3) offers another good example of price overtaking time during a sudden and extended price move. The S&P was displaying some weakness as it closed on

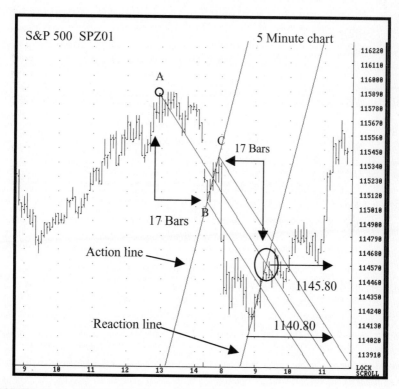

FIGURE 14.3 When Is the Price Right? S&P 500

1. The S&P breaks out of the Reaction swing of B to A and drops 1,100 points in 55 minutes. The S&P reaches the Reaction line before the predicted reversal time period.

2. After reaching the Reaction line, the S&P turns higher and reaches the center line on the predicted Reversal bar. By exiting the short trade at the Reaction line, you would have enjoyed an exit price 500 points better than exiting at the projected time.

the low (B). The next morning an attempted rally failed 20 minutes after the open (C). The next price bar confirmed the bearish Reaction swing.

I can now overlay the Action/Reaction lines and get a good idea of a price target. The reverse count from B to A equals 17 bars. The forward count indicates the pending price move should last about 85 minutes (17 bars × 5 minutes = 85 minutes). However, the market falls harder than expected and reaches the Reaction line in 55 minutes. It's now time to exit the short position and put the money in the bank! The S&P dropped over 11.00 points in 55 minutes.

The market reached the Reaction line even though the projected reversal was not due for another 30 minutes. During the next 30 minutes, the market rallied back up to 1145.00 to reach the center line. At the center line, the market formed a new Reaction swing, and this marked the beginning of a new upswing in the S&P 500.

When the market gives a profit opportunity like this, take it! You can always get back in the market and often at a better price.

February Heating Oil

The next example illustrates a very important point that a wise trader once made: "Amateurs look for perfection; professionals look for performance." Right now you are probably asking yourself, "What does he mean?" The Heating Oil example illustrates this point.

February Heating Oil was in an extended bull market, as shown in Figure 14.4. A Reaction swing had been identified as C to D and then the Action/Reaction lines were drawn. The reverse count from C to B equals 54 bars. This projects a potential Reversal date 54 bars forward from the low at D.

Heating Oil breaks out of the Reaction swing of C to D and trades in a tight upward channel. The market is stronger than expected and approaches the Reaction line in only 35 days—way ahead of schedule. Now here is the dilemma. Do I take profits now because the market is so close to the Reaction line, or do I hang on to the Heating Oil until it reaches the Reaction line before exiting? At a decision point such as this, I remember this statement: "Amateurs look for perfection; professionals look for performance."

What this means is do not sit back and think every market must develop perfectly before you act. The markets are not perfect by nature, so you should not expect perfection every time.

Whenever I approach an anticipated target price, I will give the market some wiggle room. In Figure 14.4, there is a horizontal line where the center line intersects with the Reaction line. Once the market has reached this line, it has entered into the target zone and should be watched very

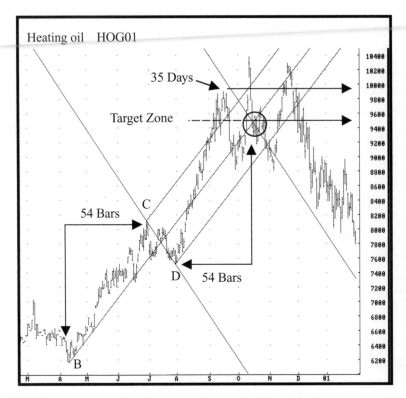

FIGURE 14.4 When Is the Price Right? Heating Oil

1. The Reversal date is due in 54 price bars from D. However, the Heating Oil approaches the Reaction line in 35 days.

2. The line drawn where the center line intersects with the Reaction line should be considered a target zone. When the market crosses through this line, it should be considered inside the target zone.

3. After approaching the Reaction line, the Heating Oil retraces to reach the center line on the predicted Reversal date.

closely. Don't reach for the very last dime! Take the money and run, as there is always another trading opportunity waiting for you.

In this example, the Heating Oil peaked at 99.00, days before the projected Reversal date. By waiting for the projected Reversal date you would enjoy potential profits, but you would also suffer huge headaches from the stress of sitting through large price swings.

CHAPTER 15

Stocks

Even though stocks and commodities are two different products, they seem to exhibit similar qualities when it comes to Reversal dates.

The stock market was developed as a means for companies to raise capital. For years, investors looked to the stock market as a place to invest for the future. The stock market was considered the safe and prudent place to build long-term wealth and security.

Commodity futures were developed to enable producers and processors to hedge their risk from fluctuating prices. The futures market offered a means of price discovery and a haven for speculators who looked to profit from the volatility offered by commodities.

DOES THE REVERSAL DATE METHOD WORK IN STOCKS?

I have used the Reversal date method in the stock index futures such as the Dow Jones, the S&P, and the Nasdaq for a long time. I have also applied the method to individual stock charts, and it seems to work just as well. Let's look at a couple of examples.

IBM

Figure 15.1 is a recent chart of IBM. The three Reaction swings illustrate the Reversal dates at work in an individual stock.

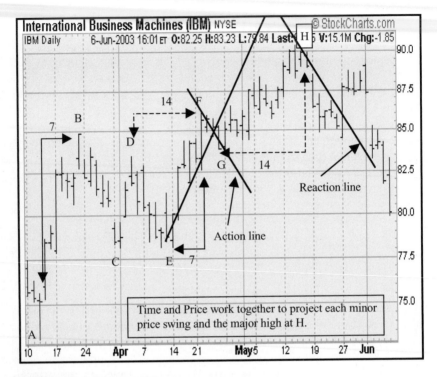

FIGURE 15.1 Stocks—IBM

1. Reaction swing C to D projects the low at E.
2. Reaction swing B to E is used to project the new Reaction swing of F to G.
3. Reaction swing F to G is used to project the major high at H.

Source: Chart courtesy of StockCharts.com

A significant low, at E, is confirmed in mid-April by the Reaction swing C to D. This Reaction swing appears inside a larger Reaction swing marked B to E. As soon as the low at E is confirmed a reverse count can be done from B to A and the future Reversal date can be projected. The reverse count from B to A is 7 days, which in turn predicts a Reversal date 7 days forward from E. Sure enough, the stock trades sharply higher into the predicted Reversal date marked F, where a new reaction swing forms.

I use the new Reaction of F to G to project forward once again. The reverse count from F to D is 14 days. Counting forward 14 days for the Reaction swing low of G, I project the next Reversal date to be due on May 15. On May 15, IBM closes at 89.90, near the 12-month high before beginning a significant correction. The market has just formed a new bearish Reaction swing.

Dell

Figure 15.2 is another example of using one Reaction swing to project another. This type of market action is most conducive to swing trading.

The reverse count from D to B equals 11 days. The forward count of 11 days accurately identifies the beginning of a new Reaction swing marked F to G.

As soon as the market moves out of this newest Reaction swing, the next Reversal date is determined by a reverse from F to D, which projects the next Reversal date to fall on May 15, marked H on Figure 15.2.

Exactly 11 days later, on May 15, the market peaks at 32.78. The next day marks the beginning of a sharp correction.

I doesn't matter whether you are trading stocks or futures in the long term or short term; Reversal dates work. As long as human emotions of fear and greed remain the same, the Reversal dates should prove useful.

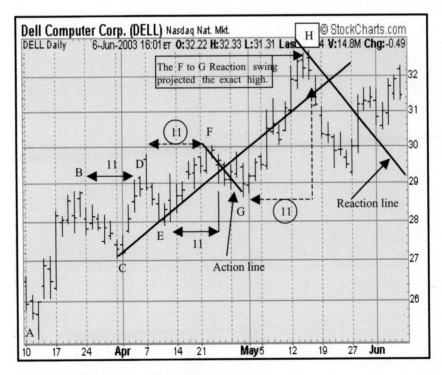

FIGURE 15.2 Stocks—Dell

Source: Chart courtesy of StockCharts.com

American Express

In Figure 15.3, the Reaction swing is in the center of the downward trend. The reverse count is 14 days. Counting forward 14 days from the high projects a possible Reversal date.

This brings up an important point that I have found useful when applying the Reversal date count to the stock market. There are times when the market will reverse one or two days after the projected Reversal date. This still puts you at a Reversal date in the correct time frame. The most important thing to remember about using Reversal dates in the stock market is that this method is highly accurate, but not infallible. The market may not reverse precisely on the Reversal date, but it will reverse within one or two days of the projected date. Just remember, no technique works 100 percent of the time.

Figure 15.3 shows how to trade this type of Reversal date situation. In a downtrend, after the market has reached the predicted date (in this example American Express is making a major low), place a buy stop above the high of the Reversal date. Leave the buy stop in place for at least two or three days. When the market reverses, the buy stop is filled and a long position is initiated at the beginning of a new bullish trend.

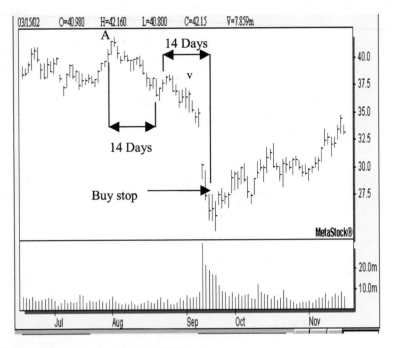

FIGURE 15.3 Stocks—American Express
Source: Charts powered by MetaStock

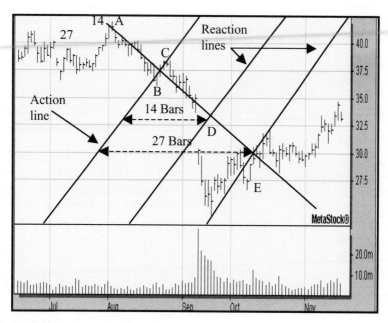

FIGURE 15.4 Action/Reaction Lines—American Express
Source: Charts powered by MetaStock

The Reversal date predictions, when combined with the Action/Reaction lines, do provide dependable timing and price signals in individual stocks. In Figure 15.4, the Action/Reaction lines are applied to the same American Express chart used in Figure 15.3.

The Action line is drawn through the Reaction swing of B to C. Next, the center line is drawn.

The reverse count from B to A equals 14 bars. The center line is marked 14 bars forward from the high at C and the Reaction line is drawn. Because the market gaps through this Reaction line, the reverse count is extended to the high of the previous Reaction swing. The count is 27 bars.

The center line is marked 27 bars forward from the high at C and a second Reaction line is drawn. The price reaches the second Reaction line at the same time a Reversal date is due.

CHAPTER 16

Knowledge Is Power

In today's marketplace, many new investors rely on someone else to make their investment decisions. I am not saying that these new investors simply hand over their money to the decision makers. The investors still have control over their money; however, they rely solely on so-called market experts for their trading recommendations without knowing the foundation or reasoning behind the recommendation.

The best investment that traders can make is an investment in themselves. If you do this, you invest in something that no one can take away from you—knowledge. This is the only investment over which an individual has complete control.

The key to helping yourself become a better trader is to know what action to take and when to take that action. Once you know that, it becomes a simple matter of following through.

The best thing is that you will have complete certainty regarding the actions you are taking. You no longer have to question or trust the judgment of others. Your decisions become easier and your trading more disciplined. Educating yourself will prove to be the best investment you will ever make.

As Benjamin Franklin said, "In this world nothing can be said to be certain, except death and taxes." This also holds true in the markets. Nothing works 100 percent of the time—but with money management, discipline, and a little hard work, you can become a better trader and gain a better understanding of market behavior.

TIME PERIODS

So far in this book, I have primarily discussed and illustrated the Reversal date concept on daily charts. I am often asked the question, "Can I use the Reversal date method to day trade?" Yes, you most definitely can! I know a professional trader who uses the Reversal date method on three-, and five-minute charts to day trade the S&P and T-Bonds. The most challenging part of day trading when using the Reversal dates is the amount of time needed to continually do the reverse and forward count.

DON'T TRY TO BE A HERO

When Holli, my youngest daughter, was six years old, her first-grade class would take one day of the week and have a "show and share" day. Once a week, the teacher would pick a letter from the alphabet and the students could bring something to class that started with the letter. This one particular week, the letter was "D." Holli gave this a lot of thought and decided she wanted to take *me* to class for show and share. Because Daddy starts with a "D," she wanted to share me with her class.

The next day, I was in Holli's first-grade class sitting on a chair so small that I could rest my chin on my knees. I watched as child after child showed off their dolls, dogs, and toy dragsters.

The teacher finally called on Holli and I was asked to join her in front of the class. Holli introduced me to the class and told them I was a broker. They were unimpressed. The teacher could sense the students' confusion, so she asked Holli to explain what a broker does. I remember thinking to myself, "Does Holli really understand what I do, and how is she going to explain it to a bunch of six-year-olds?" Holli had spent some time with me at the office on Saturdays. Even though she liked to look at the quote machines and charts on the computer while I worked, was that enough to help her now?

I was just about ready to step in and help Holli out when she said without missing a beat, "My dad sits at his desk all day and talks on the telephone while he plays computer video games with other people's money!"

Children see things as much simpler than they really are. However, there are many misconceptions about what a good broker is and the benefits brokers can offer their customers. When picking a broker, you have to remember that he or she is your employee—your broker works for you. As in any other business, the employer has to let the employee know what is expected of them. Unless you can sit and watch the markets all day long, your broker becomes your eyes and ears to the market. Remember, a broker's job is not to make you trade but to facilitate your trading. Over the years I have read about and listened to many traders and advisers saying that they never listen to a broker, as brokers are only interested in a commission. While it is true that brokers do work on commission, it is not the total focus of a professional broker who wants to remain in the business over the long term. When a broker's customer does well, the broker does well. When a broker's customer doesn't do well, the broker loses a customer. This does not benefit either one.

A qualified broker and brokerage firm can be one of your greatest assets when trading—if you do your homework when selecting them.

Almost all brokerage firms offer the same things when it comes to fast fills, Internet access to quotes, charts, and online trading at a competitive commission rate. There are only two things that can set the broker apart and above the rest: *service* and *information.*

If you are experienced and have the ability to monitor the markets all day, you may not need the assistance of a broker. However, you still need to select a brokerage firm that is willing to give you that extra service (even if you are trading through its discount division). When picking a brokerage firm, don't use price as your only qualifier. Cheap is just that—cheap! There may be times when you need help with special orders or have problems with a fill price; you want to have someone willing to help you.

If you don't have the experience, don't try to be a hero and go it alone. There is good help out there!

CHAPTER 17

Some Final Words

After you have read this material and studied the charts, you may be filled with such enthusiasm that you feel you are ready to conquer the markets. However, before you set out to do just that, I want to share with you another important rule. Never force a chart pattern or signal! Unfortunately, in our enthusiasm to be right, traders are sometimes tempted by irregular patterns and formations. Instead of waiting for the correct formation, they tend to force the trade from a pattern that slightly resembles a specific pattern. Since chart trading involves risk, even if you have a perfect pattern, using your creative imagination and wishful analysis can lead to unsatisfactory results. There are more than enough markets to trade that you will almost always find a market with an identifiable Reaction cycle about to begin or end. Remember, patience and research will be rewarded.

Always let the market tell you what it is going to do—let it do its own forecasting. If the market is not behaving as you think it should, get out and wait for the market to prove itself before reentering the trade. Once you are out of the trade, you can reevaluate the trade. It is easier to reevaluate a trade from the sidelines than from a position with a large loss. If it is still a good trade, you can always reenter. That extra commission to reenter a trade is cheaper than taking a bigger loss.

I suggest that you take the time to reread and review this book from the beginning. It is vital that you understand all the components. You need to understand the concept of the Reaction swing before you can do the reverse and forward counts. You need to understand the concept of the reverse and forward counts before you can move on to Action/Reaction

197

lines and the projection of price and so forth. Take the time to learn and practice the concepts. You will be glad you did. When you fully grasp the concepts in this book, you will never look at the market the same way as before. Imagine the confidence you will feel when you know how a market will react and unfold.

What I have written and illustrated in this book is the result of years of study, research, and experience. In the many years that I have been involved in this trading business, I have found one thing to be true: Every day is different in the market. Any actions you take and decisions you make will depend on the experience and knowledge you have acquired. This experience and knowledge will consciously or subconsciously affect every aspect of your trading.

Remember what a very wise trader once told me: "Amateurs look for perfection; professionals look for performance." Not every pattern or cycle will work or form perfectly—trading is not an exact science. All you need is confidence in the overall concept. If a pattern or cycle performs as you think it should, you are on the right track.

THE NEXT STEP

Now that you have just finished reading this book for the first time, it is time to sit back and relax. You have a lot of information to digest. For many of you, this is a completely different way to look at the markets. Therefore, take a moment to reflect—and then go through the book again.

You may have questions that the book just can't answer. This is okay—you can always pick up the phone and give me a call, or you can send an e-mail.

If you want more information you can call Traders Network at 1-800-831-7654, and I will have a complete information kit sent to you. This kit contains everything you need to begin trading: software for online trading, charts, quotes, news, and account access. Traders Network even has a tech help line.

YOU WILL NEED THIS!

Just for buying this book, you will receive the *Traders Market Views* (*TMV*). This electronic publication is sent out every Monday, Wednesday, and Friday; it is packed with the latest market information and current Reversal dates. The *TMV* is sent out via e-mail or by fax. This will allow you to compare your projections with mine—what better way to test your knowledge? Remember, if there is a question, you know where to get the answer.

You will receive this valuable newsletter for three months. This is a $90 value that is yours *free*; but first you must call 1-800-831-7654 and sign up. If you don't call you will not be automatically signed up, and you will miss a very valuable part of your education.

When you call to sign up for the *TMV*, you will receive a second bonus. You will receive a user name and pass code for the Traders Network web site. This web site is designed to meet a trader's every need. Check it out at www.tradersnetwork.com.

Evaluating Risk

Investors/traders should understand that there are risks associated with trading futures. The Commodity Futures Trading Commission (CFTC) requires that prospective customers are provided with risk disclosure statements. Historic performance results should be reviewed with the understanding that past performance is not an indicator of future results.

Resources for Traders

Trading from the Inside, by Joseph Kellogg
Tradenet Publishing Company, Loveland, Colorado,
2001

You don't have to be a Wall Street insider to trade like one! *Trading from the Inside* is a must-read for every commodity trader. Mr. Kellogg packs all he has learned about trading into this book. He breaks down trading into its components and clearly explains how to read charts, how to interpret technical indicators, and how to master trading psychology. The path to market freedom is knowledge. This book is full of wit and war stories and should be a part of every trader's library.

"I found it direct, clear, and informative. You seldom see something so successfully straightforward."

—*Stocks & Commodities* Magazine

242 pages, $49.95, ISBN 1-931611-00-9. You can order online at www.tradersnetwork.com or by calling 1-800-521-0705 or 1-800-831-7654.

The Option Traders Playbook, by Joseph Kellogg
Tradenet Publishing Company, Loveland, Colorado,
2000

The Option Traders Playbook will answer your options questions and help you develop options strategies to meet your trading goals. This easy-to-understand guide is illustrated with graphs and charts that go beyond the mechanics and the basic trading strategies of the commodities market; this guide delves into the market pitfalls to avoid. The strategies taught inside this course will open up a whole new way of looking at the futures and options markets. After taking this course, your eyes will be open, and your trading will never be the same.

175 pages, $49.95. You can order online at www.tradersnetwork.com or by calling 1-800-521-0705 or 1-800-831-7654.

TRADING TOOLS

Market Center Direct (MCD)
Online Trading Software

Market Center Direct has revolutionized futures trading on the Internet, from the live quote page and real-time data to the easy order placement and order log confirmation. Click on Bonds and instantly send a Bond order; click on E-mini and you instantly get a chart; click on Corn and you instantly get the FWN Grain news. Other built-in features include: real-time equity statements, messaging with your broker, and tracking all your orders. Market Center Direct is the ultimate trading software for active and beginning traders. With MCD, you have access to quotes from all the U.S. markets directly on your computer via the Internet.

Trade Simulator

Trade Simulator is a powerful commodity trading software tool that is built to help teach both beginners and experienced traders how to trade commodities. You will learn how to properly trade and gain "real market" experience without the risk. In just a few hours you will gain months of trading experience. Trade Simulator's database comes equipped with 17 years of real market history that covers 22 markets. Analyze daily, weekly, and monthly charts with 14 of the most popular technical indicators.

A *Futures* magazine comparison of trading simulators gave Trade Simulator the edge, saying, "It offers more indicators, more control over parameters, and it's the easiest to use."

"Overall, Trade Simulator is fun and instructive . . . [and] a good introduction to trading's decision-making process . . . making Trade Simulator a real deal."

—*Stocks & Commodities* Magazine

$99.95. Trade Simulator can be ordered online at www.tradersnetwork.com or by calling 1-800-521-0705 or 1-800-831-7654.

Traders Market Views

The *TMV* is sent via e-mail or fax every Monday, Wednesday, and Friday. Joseph Kellogg writes the "Market Scoop" section of each issue. He tells you not only what is going on in the markets, but also why—all in his own unique way. In addition, John Crane keeps you abreast of all current and upcoming Reversal day signals and patterns. Every issue is filled with valuable market information and tips. Through the *TMV* report, you will see the market in a much different way. Call 1-800-831-7654 to sign up for a free two-month trial subscription.

Appendix: Charting Basics

Here is a quick review of basic chart reading.

WHAT YOU SHOULD KNOW ABOUT BAR CHARTS

Daily Bar Chart

In a daily chart, each bar represents one day of price action. The daily record includes the high, low, opening, and closing prices. On the daily bar, the vertical line connects the high and the low (referred to as the range). There are also two small horizontal bars on the vertical bar (referred to as ticks) that represent the opening and closing prices. The opening price is the small horizontal line on the left and the closing price is the small horizontal line on the right. This bar will move one space to the right every day. See Figure A.1.

Weekly and Monthly Bar Charts

Statisticians know that the accuracy of analysis increases with the length of a study. A daily bar chart goes back only about six months. However, a weekly chart (in which each vertical line represents one week of trading) can review up to five years of activity; and a monthly chart (in which each vertical line represents one month of trading) can sometimes trace 20 years. We use weekly and monthly bar charts to look at the big picture of the price action. This compression of information helps us spot the longer-term trends. See Figures A.2 and A.3.

Trends

Prices rarely move in a straight line. Instead, the market moves in one of three directions: up, down, or sideways. A trend occurs once a market

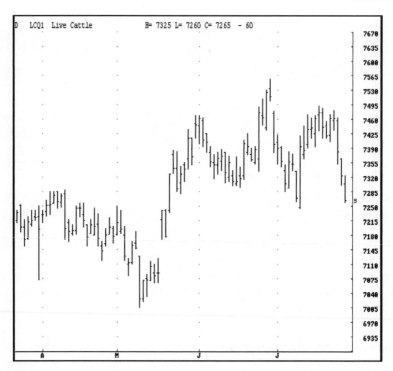

FIGURE A.1   Daily Bar Chart

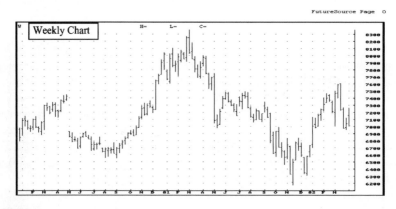

FIGURE A.2   Weekly Chart

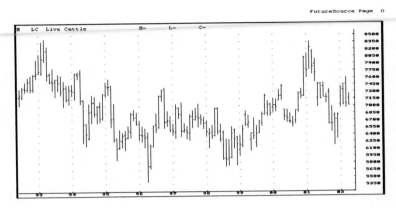

FIGURE A.3 Monthly Chart

movement establishes a noticeable pattern. Even if you study a few charts only briefly, you will clearly see that market activity usually moves in trends. In a downward trending market (Figure A.4) trend lines are drawn above the highs. In an upward trending market (Figure A.5) trend lines are drawn under the lows.

Major, Intermediate, and Minor Trends

Charles H. Dow, who was considered one of the fathers of technical analysis, classified trends into three distinct categories: the major, the intermediate, and the minor. The major trend lasts for six months to more than

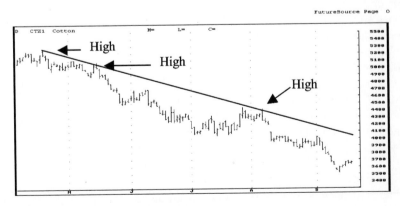

FIGURE A.4 Downward Trending Market

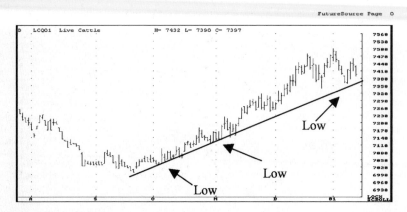

FIGURE A.5   Upward Trending Market

one year; the intermediate trend lasts for four weeks to six months; and the minor usually lasts for a few days to about four weeks. See Figure A.6.

Trend Lines and Channels

The trend line and channel line can be the most useful road maps for predicting price movements. Let's review each:

Trend Lines

The trend line defines the slope of the trend. Once this trend line is broken, an alert sounds that the market may change direction. It takes two points to draw a trend line and a third point to confirm the trend. We draw an *up trend line* under the successively higher reaction lows. We draw a *down trend line* above successive lower reaction highs. The trend line should touch the extreme high of the reaction high or the low point of the reaction low.

Channels

A channel occurs when a trend follows a straight line. The channel consists of two parallel lines that are drawn under the reaction lows and above the reaction highs. Channels also predetermine where the support and resistance will be in the trend.

Gaps

A gap is a space on the chart that is caused by a lack of trading. Generally, a gap signals the reversal of a trend. There are five different types of gaps, some of which have been discussed in this book.

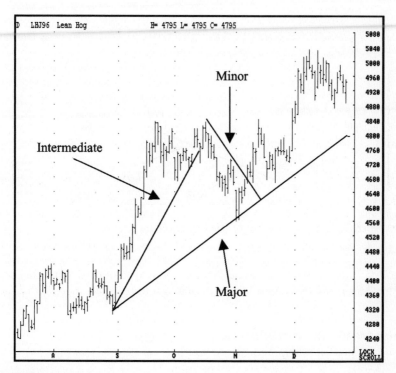

FIGURE A.6 Trend Lines

Getting Started

Before starting the trading process, you will need your own charts. These may be obtained in several different ways. There are charting companies that will send you updated charts every week. Computer programs are available that will download charts from different services. In addition, quote equipment may be acquired that updates any chart, any day, every minute.

- *Chart the closest contract month to the current date.* During your training, I recommend that you track only the contract month closest to the current date. These markets are usually the most liquid and active contract months, and therefore have the most volume and open interest.
- *Don't trade in the delivery period.* If today's date is May 5, do not trade the May futures contract month. May contracts would be in the delivery period. Instead, trade the *next* contract month available for that commodity.

- *Note the different delivery months.* In most cases, futures contracts do not trade every month. For instance, the Wheat futures trade in March, May, July, September, and December.

CHARTING TERMS

Trend   Price movement in a particular direction.

Trend line   A simple line that helps determine the direction of the trend. The duration and scope of the trend line are important factors in determining pattern reliability. Normally, three trends will move simultaneously: the minor, intermediate, and major trend lines. A trader should be aware of the direction of the three trends before entering a trade.

Minor trend   A trend that lasts for a few days up to four weeks. I recommend using a daily chart during a minor trend.

Intermediate trend   A trend that lasts between four weeks and six months. I recommend using a daily chart or weekly chart when trading an intermediate trend.

Major trend   A trend that lasts from six months to five years. I recommend using a monthly chart.

Construction of a trend line   A minimum of two points is needed to construct a trend line. When connected together by a trend line, these two points test a price pattern. The validity of the prediction increases with the number of connected points.

Upward trending market   A market in which the highs move higher and the lows move higher. The upward sloping trend line is drawn under the lowest lows of the up move.

Downward trending market   A market in which the highs continue to get lower and the lows continue to get lower. The downward sloping trend line is drawn on top of the highest highs of this down move.

Channel   A channel suggests a phase of overbought and oversold market conditions in a trend. A channel can also help to determine a minor trend reversal. Long and short positions often reverse at the location of the channel lines. The channel lines are drawn parallel to the trend line. The channel lines are drawn above the highs and below the lows of the trend. The channel lines should not cross through any highs or lows. The lines must be parallel for this to be a channel.

Risk   To reduce risk, I suggest placing a protective stop two to three points *under* the trend line for long trades and two to three *above* the trend line for short trades.

Gaps   A gap is an unfilled space on the chart. The gap occurs because there has been no trading for a period of time.

SUPPORT AND RESISTANCE

You will soon begin to notice that certain price levels attract buying (support) while others entice selling (resistance). In other words, knowing where the support and resistance levels are may help you determine your market entry and exit points.

Support and resistance are like bends in a river. They are landmarks that help you determine good places to enter and exit a market. Even though markets usually move in a wavelike motion of a series of highs and lows, the markets tend to stay within historical highs and lows. These highs and lows (peaks and troughs) are the *resistance and support* levels.

The support and resistance levels come from previous trading ranges. If a particular commodity has been trading in a price range for an extended length of time, the range becomes symbolic, as it represents an idea of fair value for that time period. Once a level of support or resistance breaks, the market moves to the next level. It searches for a new fair price and a new level of support or resistance.

Traders find support and resistance levels by studying past charts. For support, a trader will note where prices stopped going down and started moving higher. For resistance, a trader will note where prices stopped moving up and started moving lower. Traders can remember these levels through their charts. The longer that a trading range lasts, the stronger the mentality that this is a fair price. Therefore, this fair price level becomes a strong support or resistance level. Once prices move away from this range, the range becomes a support or resistance area.

Remember, it is the memory of the old range as a fair market price that reinforces this attitude. Therefore, a *pullback to support* (or the return to the old range) is a good place to buy because of its history of fair market price; conversely, a return to resistance can be a good place to sell. The more time that is spent in developing a support or resistance level, the more powerful the level becomes.

A support or resistance congestion area may appear when prices trade within a certain range for several days or longer. These congestion areas act as support in an uptrend, or as resistance in a downtrend. To determine the strength of a support or resistance congestion area, we study both the length of time and the volume of the price activity.

What You Should Know about Support and Resistance

Support and resistance levels are useful for locating entry and exit points.

- Wait until the market drops to the support level of a commodity that you expect to move higher before entering a long position.
- Wait for rallies into the resistance levels of a commodity that you expect to go down before entering a short position.

Support and resistance levels help determine the location for protective stops.

- Place a protective stop under the support level for a long position.
- Place a protective stop above the resistance level for a short position.

Penetration of a support or resistance level indicates the weakness or strength of a market.

- A penetration of a support level indicates further weakness in the market.
- A penetration of a resistance level indicates further strength in the market.

The support and resistance locations help define a trader's risk.

- Risk is the distance between the entry price and the protective stop price.

If the support and resistance levels are broken, they become the opposite.

- Broken support becomes resistance.
- Broken resistance becomes support.

Index